the complete book of
paint

the complete book of
paint

a sourcebook of techniques,
finishes, designs and projects

Lynne Robinson

Richard Lowther

Liz Wagstaff

Quadrille

p. 1: *Tones of a hue are created by adding white or umber (see pp. 30–2)*

pp. 2–3: *Chequerboard table tops with asymmetrical sections (see pp. 212–15)*

p. 5: *Stamped oak-leaf borders in three colourways (see pp. 142–3)*

The publisher takes no responsibility for any injury or loss arising from the procedures or materials described in this book. Materials, tools, skills and work areas vary greatly and are the responsibility of the reader. Follow the manufacturers' instructions and take the appropriate safety precautions.

Art Director: Mary Evans
Editorial Director: Jane O'Shea
Design: Sarah Emery
Production Manager: Rachel Wells

First published in 2000 by Quadrille Publishing Limited
Alhambra House, 27–31 Charing Cross Road, London WC2H 0LS

This paperback edition first published in 2003

British Library Cataloguing-in-Publication Data
A catalogue record for this book is available from the British Library.

ISBN 1 84400 023 0
Printed and bound in China

CONTENTS

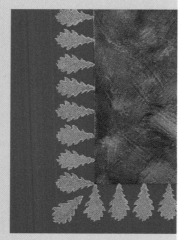

PART ONE

GETTING STARTED

Everything you need to know about materials, equipment, techniques and preparing the surface before you begin, plus special guidance on planning, choosing and changing colour and how to use the recipes.

A chequerboard table top (see pp. 212–15) in sage green and red relies on a steady hand to paint the checks on the sponged-on base coat. Artists' brushes, screw-top jars for mixing the paint, and some saucers to use as palettes are the only equipment you will need for this stage.

THE PAINT

Most of our techniques and projects have been carried out with modern, water-based paints. They are safe to work with, usually odourless and quick to dry. If you prefer to adapt any recipe to use oil-based media or traditional water-based paints such as distempers or milk paints, you must adjust the colouring material to suit (see chart) and make allowances for the differences in the way the paint behaves.

At the heart of many of our recipes is white vinyl matt emulsion. Do choose a good-quality one. Ten-litre cans at knock-down prices may be tempting, but in our experience they are loaded with so much chalky pigment that not only is the resulting finish lamentable, but it is also too absorbent. Good-quality emulsions perform well and make an excellent base for the addition of colour. When we want a dark tone, we start with a base closer to our goal – black or red, for example.

To colour the emulsion, we rely heavily on artists' acrylic colours. Although expensive compared to ordinary household paint, the quality of the pigment is high and you only need a little to bring about a colour change. Occasionally we make use of powder pigments. Unfortunately, many are toxic, especially if inhaled or handled. If you are using these, refer carefully to the manufacturers' instructions. If you decide to use vinyl silk emulsion or decorators' acrylic paint instead of vinyl matt emulsion, the colour can also be modified with artists' acrylic colours.

A few of our recipes require oil-based materials. Chosen often for their superior durability or appearance, these paints have slower drying times. This means they can be worked for longer – an advantage when creating some textural effects. As the chart indicates, oil-based eggshell and concrete paint can be coloured with artists' oil colours or powder pigment. Gloss paint is less accommodating – coarse pigment reduces its reflective quality, turning the gloss to a satin finish – and therefore we would use only tiny amounts of artists' oils to colour them.

PAINT TYPE	COLOUR WITH	THIN WITH
WATER-BASED		
• Acrylic 'milk' paint • Decorators' acrylic • 'Eggshell' paint • Floor paint • Masonry paint • Vinyl matt emulsion • Vinyl silk emulsion	Artists' acrylic colour or powder pigment	Water
• Casein/milk paint	Powder pigment	Water
OIL-BASED		
• Eggshell/satin paint • Floor/concrete paint • Masonry paint	Artists' oil colour or powder pigment	White spirit
• Gloss paint	Artists' oil colour	White spirit

EMULSION PAINTS
As well as being widely available, emulsion paints readily mix with artists' acrylic colours. Four of these swatches began life as brilliant white. The fifth has black as its base. Each has had one or more colours added to produce the hues (see p. 30) found here.

POWDER PIGMENTS
These are a way to colour paint. Their advantage is that they can be mixed with any type of paint. This can be handy if you are using a mix of media, for example emulsion for walls and oil-based paint for door and window frames. The colour range is smaller than that of artists' acrylics – you will not find neutral grey, for instance – but it does include metallic finishes (see p. 19), which the artists' acrylics do not. Once the only option for colouring paint, powder pigments are still considered the quality colour by some.

ARTISTS' COLOURS
Acrylic colours (left) are used to colour water-based materials, while oil colours are used for oil-based materials. Both are available in more hues than is strictly necessary. Buy top-quality products for the strongest pigments. Acrylics are normally sold as a thick paste, useful for stencilling, but are also available in a more fluid con-sistency. The colour is just as powerful but it is easier to apply, and it mixes more readily.

SPECIALIST PAINTS

Emulsion paint provides a fairly tough finish and, in conjunction with varnish, can be used for a surprising range of applications. Some of our floor and table top projects have emulsion paint as their base. Emulsion can also be turned into a more specialist paint by the simple addition of scumble glaze or PVA (see pp. 13 and 15).

Occasionally we have used a specialist paint to satisfy a particular need. Many of those on the market, such as colourwash, can be made at home, but one we do like is an acrylic-based paint formulated to look like traditional milk paint. It dries to a dead flat finish and, if you wish, can be rubbed back to imitate the wear and patina of an old piece of painted furniture. However, such treatment, popular though it is, belies one of milk paint's most notable characteristics – the fact that it is hardwearing and extremely durable.

Other specialist paints are sometimes needed for fitness of purpose rather than for their looks. For a well-sealed, durable painted surface on a concrete floor, we would use an oil-based concrete paint. It is specified for use on garage and car-showroom floors, so it should be capable of standing up to normal domestic wear and tear. Some of the simple wall finishes in Part Two are suitable for exterior use, and for these we suggest substituting a hardwearing, smooth masonry paint for the standard emulsion base coat. To emulate a decorative iron finish (see p. 18), we co-opt the opaque black of oil-based blackboard paint.

Artists' suppliers stock a wealth of other specialist products. Among these are glass paints, one of which is used to create stained-glass effects, while another is a frosting varnish that is an alternative to having your windows acid-etched or sand-blasted. You are unlikely to fool anyone with these products, so just treat them as decorative paints in the same way as we do.

MILK PAINTS
These are not always widely available, but they can be made at home from casein, borax and powder pigments. The result will be a breathing, non-toxic traditional paint. Modern versions – also non-toxic – are bound with acrylic.

FLOOR PAINTS
These come in a wide variety of media but not always in a wide range of colours. Here we show one bound with an alkyd resin – the most common binder for all kinds of modern household paints – reinforced with polyurethane for extra hardness. Choose a satin finish: a gloss finish will highlight any imperfections. Alternative treatments for floors include water- or spirit-based stains or coloured varnishes.

GLASS PAINTS

GLASS PAINTS
Those we use are cellulose-based. They are quick-drying, almost impossible to brush out smoothly, highly inflammable and cannot take a second coat as the solvent in the paint softens the layer of paint below. If you are prepared for all that, you can get some colourful results with them.

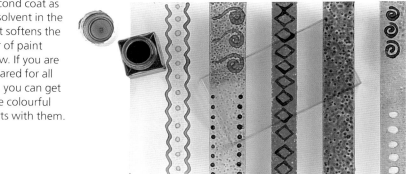

FROSTING VARNISHES
Acrylic-based, these are more user-friendly than other glass paints. They produce a convincing frosted finish when sponged on, and can be tinted or, as here, coloured with metallic and irides-cent powders. For an etched-glass look, use them with stencils or masking tape, but don't be afraid to brush or stamp them on too.

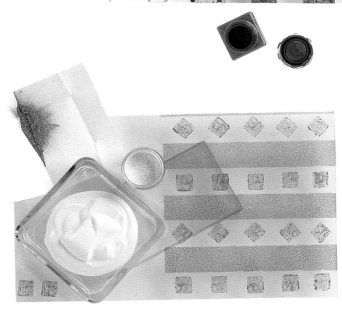

SOLVENTS & GLAZES

Most of the glaze recipes include a scumble glaze and/or a solvent. Scumble glaze is a transparent medium which extends the working time of paint, giving it permanent translucency for decorative effect. It is available in water-based and oil-based forms. Solvents also lengthen the working time; one is suitable for water-based materials, the others for oil-based. The right solvent for the job is also the right cleaner, and that applies to your brushes *and* your mistakes. Other useful thinner/cleaners include cellulose and isopropyl alcohol (see pp. 26–7).

SOLVENTS OR THINNERS

TYPE	USES	MIX WITH	TOXICITY
Water	Cleans and thins all water-based products. Also use to disperse water-based glazes for decorative effect.	Transparent acrylic scumble glaze and emulsion paint to create glazes or with acrylic varnish	Toxic when mixed
White spirit	Cleans and thins many oil-based products.	Transparent oil-based scumble glaze and eggshell paint to create glazes or with gloss paint and some varnishes	High
Methylated spirits	Cleans and thins many oil-based products. Also use to disperse water-based glazes for decorative effect.	Shellac or french enamel varnish	High

WATER-ON-OIL RESIST
Water sprayed onto an oil glaze and left to evaporate leaves distinctive circles – a useful texturing technique.

DISTRESSING PAINT WITH METHYLATED SPIRITS
Solvent rubbed into a dry coat of vinyl matt emulsion will create an aged look.

DISPERSING GLAZE WITH METHYLATED SPIRITS
Although normally used with oil-based products, methylated spirits can be used to 'weather' a water-based glaze.

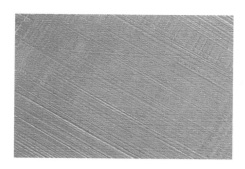

INCREASING TRANSLUCENCY
Colourwashing is a good example of the effects of scumble glaze (here the water-based form) on a glaze-mix. Parts of the base colour remain visible.

INCREASING THE WORKING TIME
Dragging requires long, continous brush strokes. Adding oil-based scumble to the glaze-mix gives you more time to work the paint before it dries.

GLAZES

TYPE	USES	MIX WITH	TINT WITH	THINNER/ CLEANER	TOXICITY
Acrylic or water-based scumble glaze (transparent)	Makes paint appear translucent and lengthens the time it can be worked. Use with water-based paint and varnish.	Emulsion paint or acrylic varnish	Artists' acrylic colour or powder pigment	Water	Medium
Antiquing patina	Ages a variety of decorative paint finishes, in particular water-based crackle.		Artists' acrylic colour	Water	Medium
Linseed oil	An ingredient of oil-based scumble glaze (see below), but also used separately to thin or extend the working time of oil colour.	Artists' oil colour	Artists' oil colour	White spirit	High when mixed
Oil-based scumble glaze (transparent)	Makes paint appear translucent and lengthens the time it can be worked. Use with oil-based paint and varnish.	Eggshell or gloss paint, or dead flat or polyurethane varnish	Artists' oil colour or powder pigment	White spirit	High

ANTIQUING PATINA
Available in umbers and siennas for ageing water-based finishes on wood.

ACRYLIC SCUMBLE GLAZE *left*
Thinned with water and used in water-based finishes.

OIL-BASED SCUMBLE GLAZE
Thinned with white spirit and used in oil-based finishes.

WAXES, POWDERS & PASTES

Waxes, powders and pastes are important, versatile ingredients in many paint recipes. Mixed with paint, oil colour or other ingredients, they are used to produce a variety of effects. Waxes also often form an essential part of the protective stage of paint finishes. Always check the chart for the appropriate solvents and thinners, as some pastes, in particular, can be difficult to remove from brushes and other equipment. Most of these materials can be obtained from DIY stores and artists' supplies shops. Store carefully and make sure all lids are secure.

WAXES

TYPE	USES	TINT WITH	THINNER / CLEANER	TOXICITY
Artists' beeswax	Soft, bleached alternative to beeswax, ideal for decorative resist work.		White spirit	High
Beeswax or furniture wax	Use for resist technique when ageing or distressing painted wood. Also polishes and seals wood. Available in pellet form.		White spirit	High
Black polish	Mix with silver metallic powder to create an iron finish. Black shoe polish (but not shoe cream) is a good alternative.		White spirit	High
Clear wax	Polishes and seals wood. Can also be tinted to darken wood.	Artists' oil colour, powder pigment or shoe polish	White spirit	High
Liming wax	Mix with whiting (see opposite) to age decorative finishes. Also polishes and seals wood.	As above	As above	High
White polish	Seals and polishes wood.	As above	As above	High
White wax	Seals and enhances wood.	As above	As above	High

BEESWAX PELLETS
Melt in a double boiler before using. Artists' beeswax is also melted but flows on more smoothly.

BLACK POLISH
Mix with metallic powder for an iron effect (see p. 18).

FURNITURE WAX
Use, like beeswax pellets (above), as a resist when ageing paint. Aerosol beeswax is a useful alternative, but avoid silicone polishes.

LIMING WAX *right*
Use for a limed effect on wood or mix with whiting to age wall finishes.

CLEAR WAX *below*
Use on its own to enhance wood or tinted to suggest the darkening that comes with age.

WHITE WAX *below*
Mix with oil colour for a tinted polish or use alone for a rich effect on wood.

WHITE POLISH *left*
Seals and reveals wood beneath light rubbed-back glazes. Also in liquid form.

POWDERS

TYPE	USES	MIX WITH	TINT WITH	TOXICITY
French chalk	See whiting.			
Sand	Gives texture and/or interest to decorative finishes, usually added to base coat and frequently rubbed back to add ageing. Available in various grades from fine to coarse, the latter usually used only with exterior paint.	Eggshell, emulsion or exterior paint	Artists' acrylic colour or powder pigment	Medium when mixed
Whiting or chalk powder	Combines with paint, PVA or liming wax for aged or dusty effects on simple finishes. Also a useful, non-waxy alternative for resist work.	Emulsion paint, PVA adhesive, liming wax or water	Powder pigment and, when mixed, artists' acrylic colour	Medium when mixed

USING LIMING WAX
Wax plays a vital part in the process of distressing the surface to create an impression of age for the simple fresco effect. After the glaze has been sanded, a layer is applied to retain the whiting, which is rubbed in to create a dusty look.

SAND
Sand of various grades can be used to give paints and glazes extra texture.

USING WHITING
Here whiting was applied to areas of detail when the paint was almost dry to suggest the crusty, weathered look of aged lead.

WHITING
Used for resist work or to add texture to simple finishes.

PVA
Mixed with pigment, it stains or seals plaster, metal and wood finishes.

PASTES

TYPE	USES	MIX WITH	TINT WITH	THINNER/ CLEANER	TOXICITY
PVA adhesive or white glue	Seals porous and flaky surfaces, such as plaster; used before water-based paints. Or use with powder pigment to stain wood.	Emulsion paint to create glaze (alternative to scumble)	Artists' acrylic colour or powder pigment	Water	Medium
EVA adhesive	The water-resistant version of PVA (see above).		As above	As above	Medium

VARNISHES & SEALANTS

These are often needed for the final stage of a simple finish so keep a variety in stock. However, besides sealing and protecting your effects against hard wear or weathering, they can play a part in the finishes themselves – either mixed with colour for the darkening that comes with age or to provide an ageing crackle effect on paint. Most varnishes and sealants are highly toxic and must be handled with care and stored with the lids well secured. Always check the drying times and follow the manufacturers' instructions for applying additional coats.

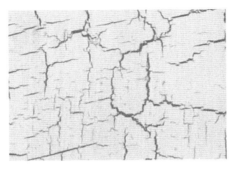

WATER-BASED CRACKLE
Used with water-based emulsion. The cracks are short and jagged. This is the varnish to choose for a stylized effect.

OIL-BASED CRACKLE
Used with oil-based eggshell paint. With wide-spaced cracks overlaying a network of hairline cracks, this is the varnish for an antique effect.

ACRYLIC VARNISH
Water-based itself, acrylic varnish is an ideal sealant for water-based finishes as it is quick drying and durable. Matt, satin or silk finishes are specified to enhance the effects.

CRACKLE VARNISH
Both water-based (top) and oil-based (bottom) crackle varnishes are used for aged effects on wood (see above). Follow the manufacturers' instructions carefully because the method can vary from make to make.

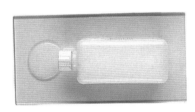

DEAD FLAT VARNISH
This produces a flat sheen for a tough sealant on oil-based finishes.

FRENCH ENAMEL VARNISH
A decorative sealant used for ornamental finishes: available in a range of colours.

POLYURETHANE VARNISH (TINTED)
Primarily for exterior use, satin and matt are most sympathetic over paint finishes.

SHELLAC *left*
Use amber shellac (or button polish) to seal gilded finishes.

YACHT VARNISH
A tough exterior-quality varnish: for use over water- and oil-based finishes.

VARNISHES & SEALANTS

TYPE	USES	MIX WITH	TINT WITH	THINNER/ CLEANER	TOXICITY	INTERIOR OR EXTERIOR USE
Acrylic varnish: clear matt, satin or silk	Seals and protects water-based paint finishes. Quick to dry and durable.		Artists' acrylic colour or powder pigment	Water	Medium	Interior
Crackle varnish	**Water based** Creates cracked-paint effect if applied between water-based base and top coats.			Water	Medium	Interior
	Oil based Creates wider spaced cracking if two coats applied over oil-based base coat.			Water (unusually)	High	Interior
Dead flat varnish	A traditional product, which seals and protects oil-based paint finishes.	Transparent oil-based scumble glaze	Artists' oil colour or powder pigment	White spirit	High	Interior
French enamel varnish	Seals and colours bronzed and gilded surfaces. Available in a wide range of colours.			Methylated spirits	High	Interior
Oil fixative	Seals cold-patination effects on metal. Also seals wood.			White spirit	High	Interior
Polyurethane varnish: clear gloss, satin or matt	Protects water- and oil-based finishes. Slow-drying and durable; gloss is the most long lasting.	Transparent oil-based scumble glaze	Artists' oil colour	White spirit	High	Exterior
Shellac (amber)	Seals and ages gilded surfaces. Also used on wood for french polishing.		Artists' oil colour or powder pigment	Methylated spirits	High	Interior
Yacht or exterior varnish: clear gloss or satin	Protects oil- and water-based paint finishes. Extremely tough and durable.	Transparent oil-based scumble glaze	Artists' oil colour	White spirit	High	Exterior

See also Clear wax and White wax (p. 14).

METALLIC FINISHES

Dutch metal leaf and metallic powders and paints, today's cheaper alternatives to real gold and precious metal leaf, have made gilding and its related finishes affordable possibilities. In many ways, these modern materials are some of the most rewarding to work with as they provide such stunning results. They are also available in many different colours and tones, giving you great scope for experiment. Take time to learn the techniques of distressing and ageing described in the recipes – they can transform sometimes harsh, tinny effects into opulence and beauty.

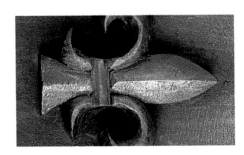

METALLIC POWDER AND WAX
Silver metallic powder mixed with black polish and rubbed in over a base coat of blackboard paint creates a convincing iron effect.

SPATTERING WITH GOLD PAINT
The least expensive form of gold finish is used for a jewel-like fantasy finish.

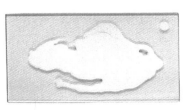

JAPAN SIZE *below*
The traditional, oil-based size, it takes a long time to dry.

ITALIAN SIZE *above*
A modern form: fast-drying, water based.

SIZES

TYPE	USES	MIX WITH	TINT WITH	THINNER/ CLEANER	TOXICITY
Italian size (water based)	Provides an adhesive, quick-to-dry base for metallic powders and leaf. Also use as a sealant on some paint finishes.		Artists' acrylic colour	Water	Medium
Japan gold size (oil based)	Provides an adhesive, slow-to-dry base for bronze and metallic powders and real gold leaf.	Transparent oil-based scumble glaze to make size more visible or oil-based paint to give a good base colour.	Artists' oil colour or powder pigment	White spirit	High

PAINTS, POWDERS & LEAF

TYPE	USES	SEALANT COAT	TO THIN SEALANT	TOXICITY
Bronze powders	Brush onto oil- or water-based size to create a metallic finish on any surface. Available in tones of bronze, gold, silver and copper. Cheaper than Dutch metal leaf and more effective than paint.	French enamel varnish	Methylated spirits	High
Dutch metal leaf: copper, gold and aluminium	Lay down on oil- or water-based size to create a metallic finish on any surface; aluminium makes an effective silver finish. Cheaper than real gold leaf. Available in whole leaves or fragments (schlag).	Amber shellac/ french enamel varnish. See also p.119	Methylated spirits	High
Gold paint or paste	Creates a gold finish on any surface. Simpler to use and cheaper than gold Dutch metal leaf and bronze powders, but not recommended for gilding.			High
Metallic powders and graphite	Brush onto oil- or water-based size to create a wide variety of coloured metallic finishes for realistic or fantasy effects on any surface.	French enamel varnish	Methylated spirits	High
Silver paint	Creates a silver finish on any surface. Simpler to use and cheaper than aluminium Dutch metal leaf, but not recommended for gilding.			High

BRONZE POWDERS
Available in a range
of gold, silver, copper
and bronze tones.
Brush onto size.

DUTCH METAL LEAF
This composite leaf
offers a cheaper but
satisfactory alterna-
tive to real metal
leaf. It is available in
many gold tones, as
well as aluminium
(for a silver effect)
and copper. Made in
sheets 15cm (6in)
square, it is also
obtainable in broken
form (schlag). The
traditional gilding
tools shown are a
knife for cutting leaf
and a burnisher with
an agate set at its tip.

SILVER PAINT
Like gold paint, this is
best reserved for
stamped decoration.

GOLD PAINT
Quick and easy to
apply, this is an oil-
based material.

GOLD PASTE
Rub or paint onto a
red oxide primer.

GRAPHITE POWDER
Add to paints and
waxes to create a
dark, 'metallic' look.

METALLIC POWDERS
Available in a great
range of colours,
they can be brushed
onto partly dry size
or mixed with wax
(see opposite) to
create a variety of
realistic and fantasy
metal finishes.

PAINTERS' TOOLS

Most of Parts Three and Four can be accomplished with a fairly ordinary collection of decorators' brushes and artists' brushes of varying sizes and qualities. We have, for example, stippled small areas with a large decorators' brush. This will be welcome news for those aghast at the price of some specialist brushes. The chart on p. 23 details specialist brushes (and their less expensive alternatives) mentioned in Part Two.

Some recipes call for a lot of brushes. We specify one for each colour. This makes for convenience but is rather expensive. In most cases you can manage with far fewer brushes by washing them out and re-using them. The sizes we give are only intended as a guide.

Water-based paints do not brush out as well as oil-based ones. Where a flat or even texture is important, we use a roller. But the cheapest means of applying paint is with a household sponge. We customize these by snipping them into shapes to match the task. This also prevents them leaving a network of straight lines in the paint.

DECORATORS' BRUSHES
Some of ours are worn old favourites that still perform well. Bottom right is a varnish brush, reserved only for varnish. In Part Two 'paint' brushes are specified. We use this vague term to indicate the least expensive, synthetic paint brushes found in any DIY store. These are used mainly for 'dirty' jobs and/or for materials which are less easy to remove after use. Water-based paint dries quickly, so always rinse paint out and wash with mild soap and water as soon as you finish. Use two pots of white spirit to remove oil-based paint, pouring enough to cover. Work off the paint in pot 1 and rinse in pot 2, removing clogged paint with a scrubbing brush. Then wash in soapy water and rinse.

ROLLERS AND ROCKERS

Rollers are an excellent way of applying emulsion. For small areas we sometimes apply the paint with a brush, then roller out the brush marks. We find the most convenient rollers are the fairly small ones with push-on heads which allow for quick clean-ups and changes of colour or texture as the job demands. Rollers will last as long as brushes if you care for them in the same way. Loaded rollers and brushes can be wrapped in cling-film for short periods. The picture also shows a rubber graining rocker. It can be rolled over a surface to create a wood-grain effect.

OTHER ESSENTIALS

Fanned out on the plate, which we use as a palette, are just a few artists' brushes – bristle flats and fitches on the right, soft-haired natural or nylon on the left. The tile is an ideal surface for rolling paint out when you are stamping. Sitting on it are two steel decorators' combs and a bunch of sponges. Combs are available in a range of different-sized teeth and widths, and are used to create ridge patterns in wet paint. Some of our sponges have had their corners trimmed, some have been cut into small balls. The tiny natural sponge is reserved for the finest of decorative effects. However, where a natural, random look is important over larger areas – in some of the simple finishes in Part Two, for example, we recommend the use of more expensive natural sponge.

CONTAINERS AND PALETTES

You will need all sorts of containers and palettes. Jars are for cleaning brushes; lidded ones are for mixing and storing paint. Paint kettles are for mixing large quantities of paint for immediate use. Plastic ones are fine for water-based paints and glazes, but a metal kettle is essential for oil-based materials. We like to mix the small amounts used in decorative painting by first stirring in a screw-top jar, then putting the lid on and shaking furiously. For mixing very large quantities you should consider upgrading to an electric drill fitted with a paint-mixing whisk. For palettes we use saucers, plates and ceramic tiles. When using these with acrylic colours, do not wash unused paint down the drain. Instead, let it dry on the plate, then soak off the paint film in hot water and throw it in a bin. Clean the steel measuring spoons and plastic jugs in the same way.

BASIC PROTECTIVE WEAR

Rubber household gloves are ideal for general tasks. For more delicate work, switch to thin latex ones. A paper mask will cut down on the inhalation of powder pigments or of dust thrown up when cleaning or sanding, but will not protect you from inhaling the harmful poisonous vapours given off by some solvents. For these you need special masks.

SPECIALIST BRUSHES

A lot of DIY stores and paint shops are now selling specialist brushes. The shape and feel of many of these make them desirable, let alone the implicit promise that here are tools which will, at a stroke, turn messy old paint into any number of fine finishes. You could, of course, tackle all our recipes with ordinary paint brushes, but for some of the broken-colour techniques in Part Two you may wish to move up a level and use a brush designed for the job in hand. Some are expensive but you can be confident that they have proved their worth over many years, are an absolute pleasure to use, and if looked after will last a lifetime. But note too that there are cheap and cheerful brushes, such as the dusting and block brushes, which can do excellent work beyond their allotted task.

SPECIALIST BRUSHES

TYPE	FILLING	FUNCTION	ALTERNATIVE
Badger softener	Very expensive, originally made from badger hair; cheaper versions now usually made from fine hog hair	Used for softening water- and oil-based glazes on walls and wood. Available in various sizes.	Dusting brush or large decorators' brush
Block brush	Inexpensive; synthetic or coarse-fibred pure bristle	First used to emulsion pebble-dash. Good for painting roughly textured surfaces and also as a cheap alternative to a stippling brush.	
Dragging brush	Flat, long, pure bristle or horse hair	Used for bold, uniform strokes on glazes and for wood-graining techniques.	Decorators' brush (see p. 20): choose one with long bristles
Dusting brush	Long, soft hog hair or cheaper filling, designed to splay out	Used for dusting surfaces after sanding. Also as a cheaper alternative to a badger softener.	
Glider	Pure bristle or thin, light squirrel hair	Used to apply oil-based glazes.	Standard flat paint brush
Stippling brush	Expensive; long, fine pure bristle, set in a wooden stock with a curved grip	Used for taking off dots of glaze for decorative effect.	Block brush
Swordliner	Extremely long, tapered squirrel hair; needs careful storage	Used for painting thin decorative lines on furniture. Also to create veins in marbling. Available in many sizes.	Fine artists' brush

PREPARING THE SURFACE

For your paintwork to look good and perform well, the surface on which it lies must be clean, free of grease, smooth, without holes or cracks, and properly primed. The chart on pp. 26–7 is a guide to the treatment of both new and old materials commonly found in the home. If the surface you are working on is not listed here, seek advice in a specialist manual or at your local DIY store.

Firstly you must clean off any dust or grubbiness. Detergent is often sufficient but must be properly rinsed off. Sugar soap also etches the surface and provides a key for the new paint. Do not swamp bare wood, fresh plaster or ferrous metals with water as they will be damaged. Marks such as grease can be removed with a solvent such as white spirit, acetone or methylated spirits.

Holes, cracks or dents must now be filled. Choose a filler to suit the surface and the size of the problem. Next, smooth the surface as flat as possible. Electric sanders produce a lot of dust and do not get into the corners. Using wet and dry paper with water gets round the dust problem, but it cannot be used with an electric sander. Some gypsum plasters, plasterboard and wallpaper cannot be sanded at all.

Finally, most surfaces must be primed to seal and stabilize them and to ensure that they will accept the paint.

BASIC CLEANING KIT
If you are painting over previously decorated surfaces, you will need a bowl, sponge, rubber gloves and sugar soap. Alternatives to sugar soap are washing soda or detergent powders. All will remove grease, but you should rinse off their residue well with plenty of clean water. Rough-textured surfaces or tough grime may also need a scrubbing brush to bring them up to scratch.

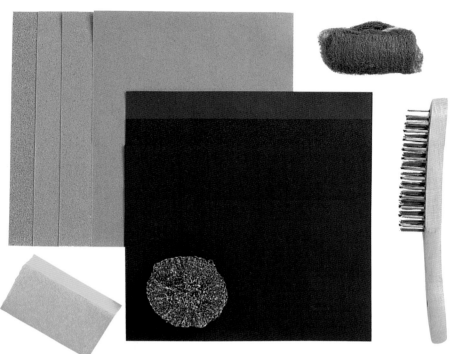

SANDING

Graded by number, abrasive papers range from 120 (coarse) to 600 (fine). Ordinary glasspaper is cheap but clogs readily. It is good for general use. Aluminium oxide paper, the yellow paper above, is superior. It clogs less readily and is less scratchy. Emery cloth is a tough abrasive for metals. All types are used dry and create dust, so take precautions and never dry-sand lead-based paint. Silicon carbide or wet and dry paper, also shown here, is the most versatile. Used wet, it does not clog or cause dust. For flaky or rusty surfaces, use emery cloth, a wire brush, wirewool or a pan scourer.

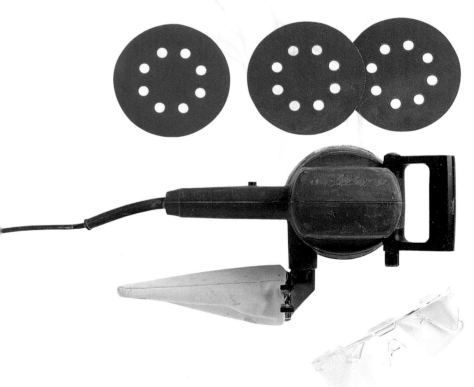

MECHANICAL SANDING

This will make short work of large flat areas. The small sander is easy to use, with its speed controls and discs attached by Velcro. It produces an excellent finish but will not deal with curves and corners. And, despite the bag, it kicks up dust.

PREPARING THE SURFACE

MATERIAL	CLEAN/ DEGREASE	REPAIR/ FILL	RUB DOWN/ SAND	PRIMER*	SAFETY
Wood including plywood and blockboard	Can be washed, but as a general rule do not wet timber – it will raise the grain and may even cause warping.	• All-purpose filler • Wood filler • Cellulose filler	• Dry-sand. Machines can speed things up. • De-nib with fine sandpaper after primer.	Knotting solution, if needed, plus: • Acrylic primer undercoat (w) • Wood primer (o)	• Dust mask • Goggles
Waxed wood	Very difficult to strip but essential or paint will not adhere. Try: • white spirit • liquid-stripping • heat-stripping • proprietary wax remover	As wood	As wood plus wirewool	As wood	
MDF, chipboard and hardboard	Wipe clean of dust and grime, but avoid getting too wet or will swell and distort.	As above. Chipboard does not have a smooth texture so spot-filling shows. Skimming the whole surface with all-purpose filler is an option if it is not a floor.	• Can be lightly abraded to give key for paint, but cannot be made smoother with sandpaper – only rougher. • De-nib with fine sandpaper after primer.	• Emulsion (w) • As wood	Dust mask
Ferrous metal e.g. steel tables	• Degrease with white spirit and wirewool or rag. • Brush down loose rust.	Plastic filler for car-body repair	• Wirewool • Wet and dry paper used with white spirit • Emery cloth	• Zinc phosphate (o) • Red oxide (o) Essential to prevent corrosion	• Dust mask • Rubber gloves • Goggles
Non-ferrous metal e.g. aluminium window frames	• Degrease with white spirit and wirewool or rag. • Wash with detergent.	As above	Wet and dry paper with water	• Etching primers (o) • Zinc phosphate (o)	Dust mask
Plaster	• Brush down. • Can be washed but allow to dry out completely before painting, especially if using oil-based paint.	• All-purpose filler • Cellulose filler • Plaster	• Dry-sand • Wet and dry paper Take care. Some plasters, e.g. gypsum, can be damaged when sanded.	• Acrylic primer undercoat (w) • Thinned PVA bonding agent (w) • Stabilizing primer (o) • Alkali-resisting primer (o)	• Dust mask • Rubber gloves
Plasterboard	Usually new so should be clean	• All-purpose filler • Cellulose filler • Plaster	Dry-sand. Use very fine abrasives and only sand the filler, not paper coating on board.	• As plaster • Thinned emulsion (w)	

* **Some of the wood finishes in Part Two – specifically Ageing Wood, Rubbing off on Wood and Woodwashing – depend partly for their effect on revealing the grain of the wood itself. For them no primer (or undercoat) is needed.**

• **Choose from the listed options. See also pp. 24–5 (cleaning/repair/rubbing down) and 28–9 (priming).**

MATERIAL	CLEAN/ DEGREASE	REPAIR/ FILL	RUB DOWN/ SAND	PRIMER*	SAFETY
Cement render on walls	• Stiff brush • Sugar soap • Detergent	• All-purpose filler • Mortar	Not possible	• Stabilizing primer (o) • Acrylic primer undercoat (w)	
on floors	As walls	• Mortar	Not needed	• Stabilizing primer (o)	
Previously painted surfaces	• Sugar soap • Detergent • White spirit Paint may be stripped with liquid stripper or burnt off.	Depends on what lies below. All-purpose filler suits most circumstances, or use filler specific to plaster, wood, metal, etc.	• Dry-sand • Wet and dry paper on sound paint and where support is non-absorbent	Unnecessary on many sound surfaces. In doubt, use acrylic primer undercoat (w) or all-purpose primer (o) Spot-prime bare patches as appropriate.	• Dust mask • Rubber gloves, mask and goggles
Papered walls	If unsound, strip off completely and treat support accordingly. It will probably be plaster. If sound, wipe clean. Vinyl paper must be stripped: it is hard to paint.	• All-purpose filler • Cellulose filler	No – except dry-sand filler	• Acrylic primer undercoat (w)	
Varnished surfaces	Treat as previously painted surfaces.	Treat as previously painted surfaces.	Treat as previously painted surfaces.	Treat as previously painted surfaces.	
Laminates and plastics	• Sugar soap • Detergent • White spirit	Plastic fillers for car-body repair	• Wet and dry paper • Coarse emery cloth	• Metal primer, followed by acrylic primer undercoat if using water-based paint	• Rubber gloves
Fibreglass	As plastics/ laminates	As plastics/ laminates	As plastics/ laminates	As plastics/ laminates	Dust mask
Glass and glazed ware	• Detergent • Methylated spirits			Glazed tiles can be primed with tile primer (w)	
Terracotta	• Stiff brush • Detergent	All-purpose filler	Dry-sand	• Acrylic primer undercoat (w) • All-purpose primer (o)	Dust mask
Cork tiles unvarnished varnished	• Detergent • Sugar soap		• Sand lightly • Wirewool	None None	

(w) = water-based   (o) = oil-based

PRIMERS & UNDERCOATS

A primer will be needed on most bare materials or on surfaces which are unsound. It provides the right foundation for subsequent coatings and prevents the paint peeling or becoming blemished. Choosing the right one is clearly essential to the success of any paintwork and the choice will depend on the underlying surface: a rust inhibitor for metal, for example, or a stabilizing solution for dusty plaster. In general most primers will accept any subsequent coating. As for the paint you use afterwards, there is certainly no problem in applying oil-based paints over water-based primers and in most cases you can put a water-based paint over an oil-based primer. What makes paint stick is a good key with no grease or dust. Our chart lists choices but it is always wise to follow manufacturers' guidelines. One other consideration is the decorative effect you are after. If this involves transparency or rubbing back to reveal what is underneath, colour your primer appropriately.

Undercoats may be needed with traditional gloss paint. This can be quite transparent and the undercoat is there to hide all unevenness of colour as well as to provide the perfect surface for a single topcoat of gloss. It may serve as a primer too so check the can before buying.

WOOD PRIMER
The ideal foundation for oil-based paints on wood, wood primer is available in pink and white.

ALL-PURPOSE PRIMER
A good sealant for a variety of surfaces, including those in doubtful condition, this is a useful item for your store.

METAL PRIMER
This primer prevents corrosion under oil- and water-based finishes. Also available in grey or pink.

RED OXIDE PRIMER
The classic metal primer, it also gives a good base for gilding and bronzing effects.

STABILIZING PRIMER
A useful primer for less than perfect walls, this binds flaky and porous surfaces.

PRIMERS & UNDERCOATS

TYPE	USES	THINNER/ CLEANER	TOXICITY	INTERIOR OR EXTERIOR USE
PRIMERS All suitable for use under water- or oil-based paints unless otherwise stated				
GENERAL				
Acrylic primer undercoat or universal acrylic primer	Seals any unpainted porous surface and patches broken areas on painted surfaces.	Water	Low	Both
All-purpose primer or universal oil primer	See acrylic primer undercoat for function. This is the primer to use when in doubt about a surface or its condition.	White spirit	High	Both
METAL				
Etching primer	For ferrous and particularly non-ferrous metal. Some types can be painted over at once; others need an appropriate metal primer (see below). Both contain acid to create a suitable key for paint.	Isopropyl alcohol (available from pharmacies)	High	Both
Metal primer	Provides a stable base for painting metal and prevents corrosion. Lot of options, depending on type of metal (steel, iron, aluminium, copper, zinc, tin or bronze), its finish (galvanized or anodized), and its condition (clean or rusty). See also red oxide and zinc phosphate metal primers.	Varies according to type: see manufacturers' instructions		Both
Red oxide primer	Prevents metal corrosion; the better option when using dark colours. Also a good base colour for gilding and bronzing.	White spirit	High	Both
Zinc phosphate metal primer	Superior rust-inhibitor, developed as an alternative to the traditional highly toxic red lead primer. Suitable for all ferrous and non-ferrous metal surfaces.	White spirit	High	Both
WALLS				
Alkali-resisting wall primer	Designed for chemically unstable lime or cement walls showing effects of alkali attack.	White spirit	High	Both
PVA solution or bonding agent	General-purpose adhesive mixed with water or emulsion for a resilient primer and sealer on unpainted plaster and other porous surfaces.	Water	Low	Interior
Stabilizing primer	Binds highly porous, powdery, old surfaces, such as limewash, distemper, cement and plaster.	White spirit	High	Both
WOOD				
Knotting solution	Seals knots and sap streaks in bare timber, especially pine. Dries quickly.	Methylated spirits	High	Both
Wood primer	Seals wood.	White spirit	High	Both
GLAZED WARE				
Tile primer	Formulated to provide a base for painting on glazed tiles, glass and melamine. Not recommended for floors.	Water	Low	Interior
UNDERCOAT				
Oil undercoat	Heavily pigmented paint which dries to matt finish. Designed for use under gloss paint to provide body and colour. Use a lighter tone than finish coat. Normally applied over suitable primer, although some are dual purpose.	White spirit	High	Both

COLOUR INSPIRATION

If, as we suggest, you are to side-step the impositions of the paint manufacturers and blend your own colours, you need to be able to predict what might happen. It is encouraging to know that colour can only be changed in three ways.

Wishing something paler is wanting a change of *tone*, and is most commonly achieved by the addition of white. To go darker, we may add black, but often raw umber is a better choice, giving softer, more natural tones. To reduce a colour's brightness means changing its *intensity* or *chroma* without changing its tone. Adding grey will achieve this, but match the grey to the colour – a dark one for dark colours and a pale one for light colours. To change red to orange – in other words to change the red's *hue* – add yellow. Attempting to change to a particular hue may not be possible, though. For instance, changing red to purple by adding blue is particularly problematic.

When choosing colours to use in combination, it is useful to limit yourself to a single hue and only vary the tone within the design. Or colour a design with only three or four hues, all of the same greyness or intensity. Working within disciplines such as these will prevent you creating visual pandemonium, while you won't fall into the trap of being too timid and painting your walls antique white.

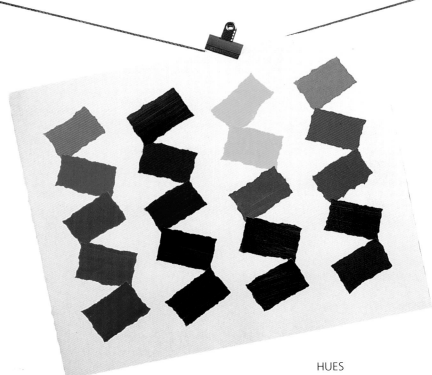

HUES
Reds, blues, yellows and greens are all different hues. In theory you can mix two primary hues together to make oranges, greens and purples, but in practice it is better to buy these colours if you want pure, intense pigment. This applies to the earth colours too.

TONES

Tones or tints are achieved through the addition of white to a hue. To make a shade, you can add black as we did to this blue, but with some colours this may also result in a change of hue. Here, as well as being made paler with white, the ochre has been gradually toned down with raw umber, and the red with burnt umber.

INTENSITY

When you want to subdue a colour without changing its tone, add grey. The grey may be bought in, or mixed from black and white. Intensity will always be reduced too when you add other hues, especially the earth colours. Colours which contain grey or an earth colour form the basis of many of the recipes given in Parts Three and Four.

COLOUR INSPIRATION

WHITE BASE
This group of recipes all start with white emulsion. Some of them include greys, some earth colours, some both. The swatch on top has had yellow ochre and ultramarine added, while the next is the white with yellow ochre and payne's grey. The third mix is with dioxazine purple and payne's grey, the fourth with raw sienna and magenta, and the last is the white plus cadmium yellow.

GREEN BASE
These swatches show how powerful a pigment phthalocyanine green is. You only need a little in any mixture, and even then the colour may be too garish. On the right of this trio, the green has been subdued with raw umber, while on the left it has been darkened with payne's grey. In the centre, it has been made paler with white.

YELLOW BASE
If you try to darken cadmium yellow with, say, payne's grey, it will turn towards green as shown on the left of this trio. Instead, try one of the earth colours such as raw umber, as seen on the right.

BLUE BASE
Cobalt blue mixed with yellow ochre and white produces a subdued grey blue which may be surprising as you might expect a green to be the result. However, the ochre is close to orange, while the cobalt blue leans towards violet. Mixing these almost complementary colours will always result in a grey. The pure cobalt on the right is modified with increasing amounts of ochre.

Adding colours to one another will bring about a change of hue, tone or intensity, and possibly all three (see pp. 30–1 and opposite). Follow the instructions in Parts Two to Four carefully for successful mixing with the minimum of wastage. In Parts Three and Four, where colour matching is especially important, we have ensured that our colour-mixing is as predictable as possible by mostly using artists' acrylic colours made from a single classifiable pigment. Each pigment has a reference number, and high-grade paints should give details of the pigments they contain. Thus mars red is in fact, PR101, a single pigment sometimes called red oxide or venetian red.

The order of mixing is important when creating a glaze. Always add the thinner (water for water-based paint, and white spirit for oil-based paint) last and slowly. It is easier and less wasteful to add more thinner than to correct a runny mix with more paint or scumble glaze.

Always test for colour and consistency before applying paint or glaze to a surface. It is much easier to adjust tone, intensity or mix at this early stage. Old pieces of wood, plasterboard or thick card make ideal test boards; keep some primed with white paint for the purpose. To test the effect of a glaze coat accurately you must apply a coat of the appropriate base colour and any previous glaze specified first. When checking wood washes, try to test on wood of a similar type and grain.

Colour correction is simple if you follow the instructions on mixing. Add all colours slowly, checking the effect as you work, but take particular care with dark hues (maybe adding them last) and with all pigment colours (they are particularly intense) or you will waste a lot of white paint or colour adjusting to the tone you want.

If a glaze does not move well when tested or lacks the characteristic translucent appearance, try gradually adding more of the appropriate scumble glaze.

Correcting mistakes of technique is always difficult. Oil-based paints and glazes dry slowly and can, with care, be wiped off with lint-free cloth soaked in white spirit. Remember to wear gloves and disturb as little of the surface as possible. With water-based paints and glazes you have to act quickly, wielding a water-soaked sponge or cloth, but be prepared to paint another base coat and begin again.

Do not forget, especially if you are using powder pigments, oil-based paints or solvents, that these are very toxic substances. Wear gloves and dust masks and do not smoke, eat or drink while working.

Apart from health risks, paint can mess up the environment. Protect the immediate one by spreading newspaper and dustsheets, but when disposing of solvents and unused paint, don't forget the wider one. If you wipe and scrape as much paint as possible off equipment when cleaning up, you will need less solvent and so create less damage to the environment. Dispose of solvents properly and remember that oil-based paint and solvent-soaked rags are inflammable.

PLANNING A DESIGN

A little forethought will enable you to carry through your ideas effectively. If you are working on a large wall or floor, take a good look at it and note the position of any architectural details, for instance doors and windows, that will have to be included in your design. Consider such things as the height of your planned border in relation to the windows in the room, the position of light fittings and sockets if you are contemplating stripes on your wall, or how to fit a repeat pattern across a chimney breast without ending up with incomplete motifs at either side.

It may help to sketch your design out on graph paper. If you work in metric measurements a scale of 1:10 is handy as 1m is represented as 10cm. A scale of 1:12 will be easier to work with if you are using imperial measurements. With a scale of 1:10, a wall 3.2 x 2.7m (10 x 9ft) would be drawn to 32 x 27cm (12^3/$_5$ x 10^3/$_5$in).

This same wall is 8.6m^2 (90ft^2). A litre of emulsion can cover up to 15m^2 (161ft^2), so if the wall includes a window or a door, you will be able to coat it twice, but it all depends on the thickness of the paint and the absorbency and texture of the wall. Tins of paint and primer always carry information on coverage, so take a list of dimensions with you when you go shopping. Our recipes specify what area they will cover.

PLANNING
Once you have chosen your motif, you must plan out your design. Plenty of graph paper, a long ruler, set square, pencils and a calculator are the basic kit you will need. Once you have drawn up a scale plan that fits, you will be ready to mark it out on the surface you are decorating.

MARKING OUT POSITIONS

As you work, you will need to mark your surface with centre lines, horizontals and registration marks. If these are not to be covered by paint, they must be temporary. Masking tape is useful for this as it can be written on. Water-soluble crayons are also handy as the marks they make can be wiped off most non-absorbent surfaces. As a precaution, though, use a crayon to match the paint you will be using.

To rule long, straight lines, stretch out a length of string, securing it with nails or masking tape. Or use a builders' chalk line. Stretch its chalky string tightly between two points and pluck it to snap a line on floor or wall. Horizontals and verticals can be ruled with a spirit level at least 1m (3ft) long. But there is also the school of thought that says you must line up designs with floors and ceilings even if these are not completely straight, and we would not disagree with that. If the layout looks right, go ahead and start painting.

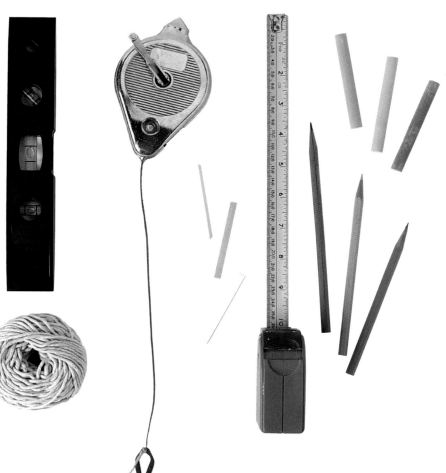

MARKING
Tautly stretched string makes an excellent guide which will not harm the surface, nor will the builders' chalk line which doubles as a plumb bob. If you have to draw on your surface, choose pencils for a wooden surface, and artists' water-soluble crayons for non-absorbent ones. Chalks are good for rough layouts and tracing down designs (rub onto the back of the design and then trace it onto the surface). All can be erased or wiped off.

SPIRIT LEVEL
Small spirit levels are useful in tight spots, but a longer one is best for ruling horizontals or verticals.

STENCILS

Essential equipment for making stencils are a scalpel or craft knife and a cutting mat. Access to a photocopier will save you having to trace and transfer. Stencils can be cut from card, paper or plastic. If they are to be used repeatedly, we use oiled manila stencil card. The oil makes the card more durable and also easier to cut.

Photocopy the image you want at the size you want, then stick it to your card using repositionable spray adhesive. Repeat patterns will be a lot easier to line up and register if you place your image at the centre of a square or rectangular piece of card. Cut through both photocopy and card with the scalpel. Be firm and try to cut in a single stroke. For a softer edge, tear the shape out rather than cut it. We sometimes use acetate sheet. This has the advantage that you can photocopy a design directly onto it.

MATERIALS FOR STENCILS
Top left is a stencil torn from oiled manila, and alongside it, one that has been cut with a knife. Images need be nothing more than photocopies of leaves, held in place on the card with repositionable spray adhesive, then cut through to make the stencil. Use masking tape to mark the positions of your stencils on the wall, and spray adhesive to hold them in place without damaging the surface while you stencil. Take great care when using spray adhesive. It is highly toxic.

2 With the stencil still in place, sponge in a second colour along the bottom edge and part-way up the side. Once most of the paint has left the sponge, start moving the sponge up the motif to form a shadow, its colour fading gradually away. Add some of the same colour to the stalk as well.

1 Hold the stencil in place with spray adhesive and have ready a spoonful of acrylic paint on a saucer, and a piece of trimmed household sponge. Dip the sponge into the paint but do not overload it. Gently dab the colour into the stencil. Aim for all-over distribution of the paint but do not be too fussed about achieving an even texture.

3 Once the stencilling is completed, peel away the stencil card and allow to dry.

4 You will be left with a pair of gently shaded cherries.

STAMPS

Stamps are a quicker way of applying designs than stencils and are ideal for small, uncomplicated motifs. Most of our stamps are made from thin, foam-rubber mat of the kind backpackers carry. This is very easy to cut and holds its shape well, whilst being elastic enough to print on top of uneven surfaces. You can also make stamps from sponge cleaning cloths or flocked draining mats used for wine glasses. Experiment with whatever is available.

Cut your design using a scalpel. Work on a cutting mat to do this. The stamp must then be stuck to a backing board which should remain rigid and not warp when wet. Foam-core board, available from artists' suppliers, is quick and easy to cut. You may also use offcuts of wood or marine ply. These are cheaper and have the advantage that you can screw handles or knobs to their backs, which makes the stamping a great deal easier.

Much smaller stamps can be carved from an eraser with a scalpel. If you cannot find an eraser big enough, stick four together with superglue. These will not need a backing board.

When you are cutting your stamps, do not forget that you are making a mirror-image. Getting the motif the wrong way round may not be too serious for many of the projects in this book, but if you intend to stamp any lettering, make sure you get it right.

MATERIALS FOR STAMPS
Foam rubber is cut to shape and stuck to a backing board with contact adhesive. For complex shapes, trace the design onto paper, cut it out and use as a template to draw around with a fine waterproof felt-tip pen. For a mosaic effect, make stamps from small pieces of foam rubber glued to a backing board. For a two-colour motif, use two interlocking stamps, as shown here.

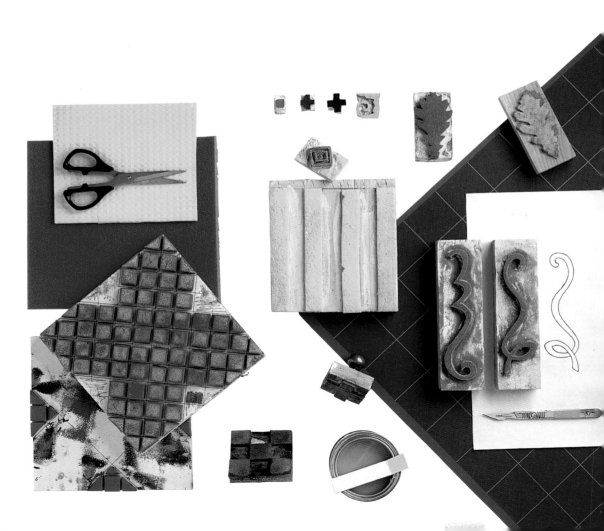

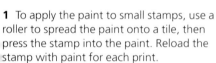

1 To apply the paint to small stamps, use a roller to spread the paint onto a tile, then press the stamp into the paint. Reload the stamp with paint for each print.

2 Place the stamp in position along a guideline which can be masking tape, as here, or a stretched-out string, then press down firmly. The wooden backing board is thick enough for you to grip comfortably with your fingers.

1 This larger stamp has the paint applied to it directly with a roller. This roller is made of sponge covered in flock and was originally designed for painting behind radiators.

2 Test your stamp on a piece of paper before you start work to ensure that you are applying pressure equally to all sections of the motif.

MASKING OUT

We find masking tape indispensable. Because it does not stick permanently to a surface, it can be used in all sorts of ways – holding stencils in place, attaching colour swatches and sketches to a wall, marking height lines, centre lines, and so on.

It is sold in a number of forms. The ordinary type is good for masking off windows, floors and all those fixtures which you would otherwise have to paint around very carefully. Mostly though, we use it within a design to prevent paint from drifting into the wrong area, or to create stripes or smart finishes to the edge of a shape. However, ordinary tape can pull a paint film off if it is very fresh or has been applied to a poorly prepared surface. Manufacturers now make tapes for delicate or freshly painted surfaces, but do test them out in an unobtrusive place before pressing them into service. Another specialist tape is one that will follow a curve, made from a wrinkly crepe paper.

Some techniques and projects in Parts Three and Four require you to mask off well beyond the shape you are working on. This can be done by sticking till roll alongside thin tape, rather than by buying wide tape. If you use double-sided masking tape, this is very easy to do.

Till roll and paper can also be turned into masking with the aid of repositionable spray adhesive. And tape and paper can all be torn to give a softer edge to a design rather than the super-straight one which you usually get with tapes.

MASKING TAPES
This selection of masking materials includes masking tape which can follow a curve, as well as a blue tape for use on delicate surfaces. The tape for delicate surfaces is very flat, allowing almost no seepage of paint underneath if it is well applied. Till roll and everyday parcel paper can also be made into masks.

1 Tear till roll along its length, spray it with repositionable spray adhesive, and use to mask out a cross.

2 Apply the paint with a small roller, taking care not to press too hard and force paint underneath the masking.

3 Slowly peel the masking away. The uneven edges left by the torn tape leave a soft, natural look.

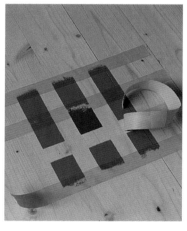

1 Lay out a grid of masking tape, pressing it down well, then sponge undiluted colour evenly into the exposed squares.

2 With careful sponging, it is possible to colour individual squares differently.

3 Once the paint is touch-dry, peel the tape away to reveal a crisp-edged motif.

1 Use a combination of till roll and masking tape to mask off alternate stripes on a colourwashed background, then apply a second colour using a roller.

2 Wait until the paint is touch-dry, then carefully peel off the masking to reveal colourwashed stripes.

MORE MASKING OUT

Masking can also be used to draw and shade motifs. Ordinary masking tape can easily be torn along its length, and strips of torn tape can be built up into attractive, angular motifs. Tape designed to go around curves makes for curvilinear designs. When you use it, ensure it is well stuck down. Because of the wrinkly, stretchy nature of the paper it is made from, it can suffer from paint seeping behind it. If you sponge over using dryish paint, that will help to avoid this problem. Masking can also be made from torn card. We have used it here to add some shading to a motif.

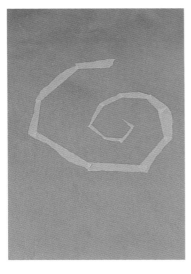

1 Tear small strips of tape along their length and stick them down in a spiral with their ragged edge facing outwards.

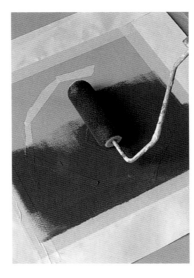

2 Use more tape and till roll to mask off a square around the spiral. Apply the colour with a roller.

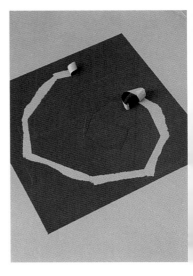

3 Once the paint is touch-dry, carefully remove all the masking to leave behind an angular spiral on a square. You could 'tile' a whole floor in this way.

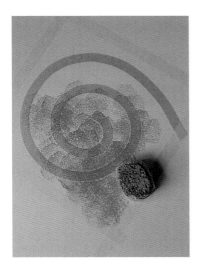

1 Stick masking tape for curves firmly down on a line drawn with water-soluble crayon. Mask off a square around the spiral. Sponge the colour on lightly but evenly using dryish paint.

2 When the paint is touch-dry, slowly remove the tape.

3 Remove the rest of the masking and you will be left with a spiral design on a square.

1 Mask off a square. Sponge lightly all over in red, then use a torn strip of stencil card to mask across the diagonal. Sponge again in red on one side of the diagonal.

2 Use a second torn strip of stencil card to mask across the other diagonal and sponge lightly in blue.

3 Using both strips together across the diagonals, sponge in the final section in a solid blue.

4 Your finished result will appear to be a pyramid with each face illuminated in a slightly different manner.

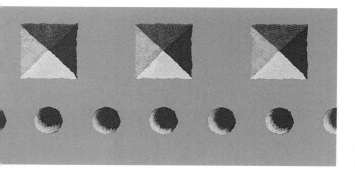

5 This technique was used to make the stencilled border on p. 159.

PART TWO

SIMPLE
FINISHES

Traditional and contemporary finishes for walls, finishes to make all kinds of surfaces look like wood, stone and metal, plus ornamental finishes for that decorative final touch.

A contemporary look for a paint finish with a past (see p. 85). Paint has been aged for centuries to lend stature to humbler pieces of furniture, but there is more than a hint of irony in the choice of brightly contrasting colours and the emphatic use of ageing for this new table of doubtful parentage. The wall has been colourwashed and rubbed back in similar tones (see p. 48).

INTRODUCTION

Paint has been used for centuries to decorate all kinds of homes and in that time a huge variety of finishes and effects have been employed beyond the flat coverage of a simple painted surface.

Many of what are now regarded as traditional paint effects have their origins in the great houses of the European aristocracy and were later adopted by the rising merchant classes who wanted to share in those splendours themselves. In the Middle Ages in Italy, for example, it was the fashion for merchants to commission artists to paint 'hangings' on their walls to simulate the opulence of fabrics they had seen abroad. And the skilled art of dragging was developed in eighteenth-century France by those with more taste than money who wished to enjoy the look of silk-lined walls.

Transformation, illusion, or more frankly deception, was usually the guiding principle. As early as the fourteenth century, for example, the art of gilding – applying thin layers of gold to surfaces such as wood or plaster – became an immensely popular way of imitating the real gold decoration which only the richest could afford. Similarly, a trend for simulating marble began during the Renaissance in Italy and France, though in time marbling techniques became enormously sophisticated, with some painters developing fantastical colours instead of realistic greys and pinks and yellows.

The opening of the silk route from China to Europe had a profound effect on the history of paint finishes, too. Items decorated with inlaid shell were traded with Europe and by the sixteenth century Italian craftsman had found a way to repeat the effect and were inlaying shell using pewter. The following two centuries saw French, Dutch and German craftsmen using the same methods to produce fine *objets d'art* and furniture. Inlaid tortoiseshell, in particular, was highly prized, but demand outstripped supply so a simulation technique was developed, reaching the height of its popularity in the late seventeenth century.

The eighteenth century also saw the development of other stone finishes with the fashion for simulating the look of exterior stonework inside the home. At first the finishes were used on large areas and architectural details. Later, they were scaled down for smaller rooms and less grand objects.

The need to transform or simulate materials continues to the present day in the techniques used to produce theatrical scenery and properties. With limited budgets and tight deadlines, these tend to be economical, simple and quick-drying.

Today great houses may have the best preserved examples of traditional paint finishes, but there are other good examples of wonderful effects in much simpler public buildings and in homes and apartment buildings all over the world, because alongside the grand tradition there has always been the vibrant legacy of folk and popular style – demonstrated in this collection of recipes by, for example, the cool blue-grey colour palette of the traditional Scandinavian interior and the sober tones of the Shaker community in the United States. These are styles and finishes firmly rooted in the often harsh climatic, economic and/or social realities of a particular region, perpetuated over centuries by people for whom the concept of style has often, for one good reason or another, been meaningless.

Many of the materials used in the past are still available and experts working on great old buildings and antique funiture undertake restoration work using the same equipment and techniques. However, for less elevated interiors modern substitutes can work well, and, as the results are quicker, materials are less toxic and many are available in a wider range of colours, they offer an attractive alternative.

You have in Part Two a battery of traditional and contemporary effects that will enable you to undertake projects in any number of different styles. Remember too that these simple paint finishes can do far more than change the colour of a room. We all now recognize how cool blues and warm reds can transform a room's mood, but take that a stage further and clever use of colour can transport you to other countries and climates. What could be more Mediterranean than those sun-bleached blues? Paint finishes can also revive some favourite memory. For example, a room that reminds you of the sea on sunny summer mornings might be achieved with the translucent glazes of colourwashing.

We hope these recipes will also open up for you the possibilities of painting furniture and other objects. Old or commonplace furniture can so easily take on a new personality, and new, utilitarian pieces that lack life and interest can be fun to age and distress. The latter may seem like madness at first, but the right paint finishes can lift a piece that might otherwise have been simply commonplace into something unusual and genuinely individual.

Eventually you will feel able to adapt the recipes for yourself. Mixing your own colours also adds another dimension, for you can match almost anything from a dish of butter to a leaf picked up on a country walk. After all, if the results are not satisfactory, a surface can always be painted again with a different colour or a different finish. Remember, too, that with a little hard work almost any surface, however poor, can be prepared for paint.

There really are no limits to what you can do. So have fun with texture and colour as you experiment with the wide range of finishes open to you. Go wild with those sponges, spatter, stipple and rub down to your heart's content. When you finally rest from your labours, you will have the satisfaction of having created something extraordinary from a simple pot of paint.

COLOURWASHING

Colourwashing is among the group of finishes that have their beginnings in fine art. Called the broken-colour techniques, they all involve distressing a semi-translucent paint or glaze over a contrasting, opaque base coat to produce subtle variations of tone. Specifically, colourwashing involves the application of thin washes of glaze in which the brush marks are left apparent to give the finish texture and depth. It provides an interesting alternative to flat colour and can be used to decorate period or modern, town or country interiors. Water-based products speed up the traditional process, which uses distemper.

A terracotta colourwash was used to decorate this farmhouse. Traditionally painted in flat, pale colours or simply in white, such interiors respond well to a rubbed-in wash technique. For this effect, brush the glaze on and then rub it into the wall with a cloth, using a random action.

BASIC RECIPE – YELLOW OCHRE ON STONE

INGREDIENTS

To cover approximately 12m² (129ft²)
Base coat ▶ 1 litre white vinyl silk emulsion / 1tbsp neutral grey artists' acrylic colour / 2tbsp yellow ochre artists' acrylic colour / ¹/₂tbsp raw umber artists' acrylic colour
Glaze coat ▶ 500ml white vinyl matt emulsion / 500ml acrylic scumble glaze (transparent) / 3tbsp yellow ochre artists' acrylic colour / 2tsp vermilion red artists' acrylic colour / 1tsp raw sienna artists' acrylic colour 400–500ml water
Optional protective coat ▶ 1 litre clear matt acrylic varnish (one coat)

EQUIPMENT

2 containers / paint roller plus tray / 1 x 75mm (3in) decorators' brush large, hard-bristled decorators' brush / badger softener or 1 x 75mm (3in) soft-bristled decorators' brush / 1 x 50mm (2in) varnish brush (optional)

INSTRUCTIONS
Base coat

1 Pour the vinyl silk emulsion into one of the containers. Add the neutral grey, yellow ochre and raw umber and stir well.
2 Apply evenly to your prepared surface (see pp. 24–7) with a roller. Allow to dry (2–4 hours).

1 YELLOW OCHRE ON STONE
The basic recipe described opposite: its subtle effect works well in traditional interiors.

2 BLUE ON WHITE
White vinyl silk emulsion is used for the base coat, and the glaze is coloured with 3tbsp cobalt blue and 2tbsp ultramarine acrylic colour.

3 TERRACOTTA ON STONE
The stone base follows the basic recipe, and the glaze is coloured with 3tbsp venetian red and 1tbsp yellow ochre. A large brush stroke was used.

4 LILAC ON WHITE
This bold, modern colourway works well in traditional rooms too. The base is white vinyl silk emulsion, and just 3tbsp brilliant purple to colour the glaze coat.

5 MINK ON WHITE
A soft, neutral look for a period home or modern interior: white vinyl silk emulsion for the base, and 2tbsp neutral grey and 2tbsp bronze ochre to colour the glaze coat. Bold crosshatching was used to create the diamond effect.

6 GREEN ON WHITE
The glaze is coloured with 3tbsp bright green over a base of white vinyl silk emulsion, and a bold random brush stroke was used.

COLOURWASHING

Glaze coat

1 Pour the vinyl matt emulsion into the other container. Add the acrylic scumble, yellow ochre, vermilion red, raw sienna, and water (a little at a time) and stir well until you have a runny but not too thin glaze. The right consistency is important here – the base coat should show through the glaze in the final effect.

2 Apply the glaze coat, using a 75mm (3in) decorators' brush. Work with random strokes, concentrating on an area of no more than 1m² (3ft²) at a time. If you want a more even effect, use arc-like brush strokes instead.

3 Using the dry hard-bristled brush, go quickly over the surface again, working with random strokes in all directions.

4 Holding the badger softener (or soft-bristled brush), skim the surface lightly, just touching it with the brush. This softens the brush strokes, but take care – overdo it and you will drag the glaze. Leave to dry (2 hours).

Notes You can repeat the glaze stage if you want a greater depth of colour. Emulsion paint and scumble glaze together dry to a tough finish, but if you are colourwashing an area that will receive a lot of wear, such as a hallway, it is best to protect it with one or two coats of varnish, according to the manufacturers' instructions.

When colourwashing on wood, make sure you apply both base and glaze coats in the direction of the grain. Brush on the base coat and, when dry, rub on the glaze using a cloth. Soften the glaze coat as in step 4 above. Again, apply one or two coats of varnish if required.

Exterior use Substitute smooth masonry paint in the base coat and finish with two coats of matt polyurethane varnish.

Soft blue tones have been used to colourwash this hallway. An ideal use of a simple colour effect, it has brightened a narrow, slightly gloomy passageway, and the small amount of ochre used in the glaze mix has taken the coldness out of the end effect.

This simple MDF magazine rack has had an ochre colourwash applied over a stone base coat, following the ingredients given in the basic recipe. The freehand and stencilled decoration are inspired by the Bloomsbury style.

SPONGING OFF AND ON

Sponging is a modern broken-colour technique. Natural sponge, moistened with water or soaked in glaze, is used over a contrasting glaze or opaque base coat to produce a softly mottled effect – by either removing or adding colour. We like to combine the two methods in a versatile finish which produces both subtle and striking results: pastel hues create an airy lightness, while stronger, related colours give rich, deep tones. Use sea sponges if you can – they create more interesting textures than the uniform marks made by synthetic household sponges.

BASIC RECIPE – GREY ON STONE

INGREDIENTS

To cover approximately 12m² (129ft²)
Base coat ▶ 1 litre white vinyl silk emulsion / 2tbsp burnt umber artists' acrylic colour / 1/2tsp ultramarine artists' acrylic colour / 1/2tbsp mars black artists' acrylic colour
First glaze coat ▶ 500ml white vinyl matt emulsion / 250ml acrylic scumble glaze (transparent) / 2tbsp neutral grey artists' acrylic colour / 1tbsp burnt umber artists' acrylic colour / 1/4tbsp mars black artists' acrylic colour / 200ml water
Second glaze coat ▶ 500ml white vinyl matt emulsion / 250ml acrylic scumble glaze / 2tbsp mars black artists' acrylic colour / 1/2tbsp burnt umber artists' acrylic colour / 250ml water
Optional protective coat ▶ 1 litre clear matt acrylic varnish (one coat)

EQUIPMENT

3 containers for mixing paint and glaze / 2 x 75mm (3in) decorators' brushes or 1 paint roller / roller tray / sea sponges in various sizes / water for dampening and rinsing sponges / disposable gloves / 1 x 50mm (2in) varnish brush (optional)

INSTRUCTIONS
Base coat

1 Pour the vinyl silk emulsion into one of the containers. Add the burnt umber, ultramarine and mars black and stir well.
2 Apply evenly to prepared surface (see pp. 24–7) with a 75mm (3in) decorators' brush (or roller). Allow to dry (2–4 hours).

First glaze coat

1 Pour the vinyl matt emulsion into a second container. Add the acrylic scumble, neutral grey, burnt umber, mars black, and water (a little at a time) and stir well.
2 Apply an even coat of glaze using a 75mm (3in) decorators' brush and covering the base coat completely. (You can use a roller if you prefer, but only for large areas.)
3 Immerse one of the sponges in water and wring out until almost dry. Put on the gloves and apply it to the surface, partially removing the glaze with soft dabbing movements. Vary your wrist position to create a variety of effects and strokes. You can also create varied effects with sponges of different sizes. Allow to dry (1–2 hours.)

Second glaze coat

1 Pour the vinyl matt emulsion into a third container. Add the acrylic scumble, mars black, burnt umber, and water (a little at a time – this glaze must be more watery than the first). Stir well.

2 Pour a little of the glaze into the clean roller tray, topping up as required. (Small quantities reduce the risk of overloading the sponge.)

3 Put on the gloves and, using another slightly damp sponge, apply the glaze to the wall in light dabbing movements, turning the sponge to vary the pattern. Again, sponges of varying size will help. Rinse them in water regularly to prevent them from clogging. Allow to dry (2 hours).

Notes Apply one or two coats of varnish for a hardwearing surface, according to the manufacturers' instructions.

The combination of these techniques gives greater depth to the colour and finish but you can use either of them alone.

① GREY ON STONE
The basic recipe: an ideal treatment for a traditional interior. Above the dado rail the grey glaze has simply been sponged off; below it the same glaze has been sponged off and then on.

② DUSKY PINK ON CORAL
The coral base coat is coloured with 2tbsp cadmium red and 1tbsp raw umber, and the glaze with 2tbsp cadmium red, 1tbsp raw umber and ½tbsp neutral grey. These rich hues work well in traditional or modern interiors.

③ OCHRE ON SAND
A neutral look to complement natural fabrics: colour the base coat with 1tbsp yellow ochre and 1tbsp raw umber, and the glaze with 3tbsp yellow ochre.

DRAGGING

Developed in the eighteenth century, dragging derives from the techniques of wood graining. Translucent glaze is brushed onto a base coat and a clean, long-haired brush is drawn from top to bottom to reveal the base colour in a series of fine lines. Traditionally a dark, oil-based glaze was used and oil-based paints remain the more satisfactory medium because they dry more slowly than water-based ones, allowing for longer working, and the intensity of oil colour gives a better result. Attempt it only on smooth surfaces – lumps and bumps spoil the vertical lines.

BASIC RECIPE – OIL-BASED DEEP BLUE ON WHITE

INGREDIENTS

To cover approximately 16m² (172ft²)
Base coat ► 1 litre white oil-based eggshell paint
Glaze coat ► 500ml oil-based scumble glaze (transparent) / 2tbsp ultramarine artists' oil colour / 1tbsp prussian blue artists' oil colour / ¹/₂tsp yellow ochre artists' oil colour / 150ml white spirit
Protective coat ► 1 litre oil-based clear dead flat varnish

EQUIPMENT

2 x 75mm (3in) paint brushes or 1 paint roller plus tray / container for mixing glaze / disposable gloves / dragging brush or 1 x 75mm (3in) flat, long-bristled decorators' brush / rags / wirewool (optional) / 1 x 50mm (2in) paint brush

INSTRUCTIONS

ALWAYS WORK IN A WELL-VENTILATED AREA

Base coat

Stir the oil-based eggshell paint well and apply an even coat to your prepared surface (see pp. 24–7) with a 75mm (3in) paint brush (or roller). Allow to dry (24 hours).

Glaze coat

1 Pour the oil-based scumble into the container. Add the ultramarine, prussian blue and yellow ochre and mix well.
2 Stir in the white spirit (a little at a time) until the glaze has a milky consistency.
3 Using a 75mm (3in) paint brush (or roller), apply to the base coat, working evenly with horizontal and vertical strokes.
4 Put on the gloves and wear for the remainder of this stage. Starting at the top of the surface, use the dragging or long-bristled brush to draw or drag the glaze down to the bottom in one uninterrupted stroke. Wipe the brush clean on a rag. Keeping a check on the alignment, begin another stroke. For a rougher effect, repeat the action after each stroke or once the entire wall has been dragged. Or redrag using wirewool instead of the brush. (Wipe the wirewool clean after each stroke.) Allow to dry (24 hours).

Protective coat

Apply one coat of varnish, using the 50mm (2in) paint brush, according to the manufacturers' instructions.

❶ DEEP BLUE ON WHITE and PALE BLUE ON ULTRAMARINE The upper section illustrates the colourway and method used in the basic recipe. The lower section appears as a mirror image of the other, but different colours are used to achieve the effect. The base coat is a premixed oil-based ultramarine eggshell paint, and the glaze tone is a mix of 2tbsp titanium white and ¹/₄tsp ultramarine. It has been dragged and then redragged three or four times with wirewool. The border was stencilled with tinted eggshell paint.

❷ OCHRE ON STONE
A pale glaze dragged over a deeper base coat: a modern approach. The glaze is tinted with 2tbsp yellow ochre and 1tbsp raw umber and applied to a base coat which is coloured simply with 2tbsp yellow ochre.

❸ PALE PINK ON TERRACOTTA
The base coat is coloured with 2tbsp

yellow ochre and 1tbsp red oxide, and the glaze coat uses 2tbsp titanium white and ½tbsp cadmium red and ½tsp cobalt blue. The result: another pale on dark colourway.

❹ DEEP RED ON AQUA GREEN
The base coat is coloured with 1tbsp viridian green and 1tbsp cobalt blue, the glaze with 1tbsp

cadmium red, ½tbsp red oxide and ½tbsp burnt umber. This gives a sumptuous look.

❺ SEAGREEN ON WHITE
White eggshell was used for the base coat, and the glaze colours are 2tbsp viridian green and 2tbsp cobalt blue: a fresh colourway that works equally well in modern or period rooms.

❷

❸

❹

❺

STIPPLING

Traditionally stippling entails the reworking of newly applied paint to create a finely textured, matt finish. Glaze brushed over a different hue or tone and stippled (as here) will reveal glimpses of the colour below. A well-prepared surface is essential – the technique emphasizes any imperfection – and oil-based paints are preferable over large areas. Stippling brushes give the best results; block brushes (or shoe brushes) are cheaper alternatives. An elegant effect which adds subtle ageing to a room, it also looks good on wood panelling, furniture and frames.

BASIC RECIPE – OIL-BASED RED ON RED

INGREDIENTS

To cover approximately 16m² (172ft²)
Base coat ▸ 1 litre premixed deep red oil-based eggshell paint
Glaze coat ▸ 500ml oil-based scumble glaze (transparent) / 3tbsp cadmium red artists' oil colour / ½tbsp raw umber artists' oil colour / 1tbsp linseed oil / 150ml white spirit
Protective coat ▸ 1 litre oil-based clear dead flat varnish

EQUIPMENT

2 x 75mm (3in) paint brushes or 1 paint roller plus tray / container for mixing glaze / disposable gloves / stippling or block brush / rags / 1 x 50mm (2in) paint brush

INSTRUCTIONS

ALWAYS WORK IN A WELL-VENTILATED AREA

Base coat

Stir the oil-based eggshell paint well and apply an even coat to your prepared surface (see pp. 24–7) with a 75mm (3in) paint brush (or roller). Allow to dry (24 hours).

Glaze coat

1 Pour the oil-based scumble into a container. Add the cadmium red and raw umber and stir well.
2 Add the linseed oil and a little white spirit and mix again. Stirring all the time, add more white spirit until you have a milky but not too runny consistency.
3 Apply to the base coat with a 75mm (3in) paint brush (or clean roller), using vertical and horizontal strokes for an even finish and covering the base coat completely. If you use a brush, quickly dab the end of it over the glazed surface to get rid of any brush marks.
4 Put on the gloves and wear for the remainder of this stage. Lightly dab the stippling or block brush over the surface, using a gentle tapping action. Clean any drips with a rag. Work with the wrist rather than the arm as it is less tiring and gives a softer look. Vary the finish by changing the angle of the brush occasionally. Allow to dry completely (24 hours).

Protective coat

Apply one coat of varnish, using the 50mm (2in) paint brush, according to the manufacturers' instructions.

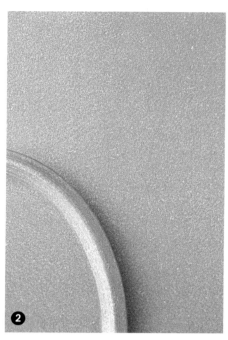

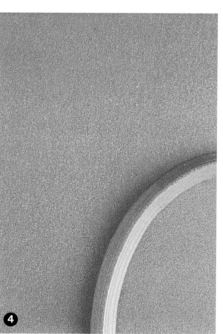

❶ RED ON RED
The basic recipe: in this classic scheme the deep red glaze appears even more intense alongside tiny flecks of the red base coat. The result is a subtle but dramatic way of executing the effect.

❷ GREEN ON GREEN
For the base coat, 1 litre white oil-based eggshell paint is tinted with 1¹/₂tbsp sap green. The glaze coat follows the basic recipe, but using 1¹/₂tbsp sap green and 1tbsp titanium white. This would be a lovely scheme for a bathroom.

❸ DEEP GREEN ON STONE
The colouring in the base coat is 2tbsp yellow ochre and ¹/₂tbsp raw sienna (stirred into 1 litre white oil-based eggshell paint). Again, the glaze follows the basic recipe, but using 2tbsp sap green and ¹/₂tbsp raw umber. These striking tones have the authority for a period setting.

❹ YELLOW ON YELLOW OCHRE
A bold colourway for a contemporary home: 1 litre white oil-based eggshell paint is coloured with 2tbsp yellow ochre to create the base, while the glaze follows the basic recipe, but using 3tbsp yellow ochre and ¹/₂tbsp cadmium yellow.

WATER-BASED STIPPLING

Apply two coats of a premixed deep red emulsion. Allow to dry (2–4 hours). Then mix a glaze using the same quantities as for the basic recipe but substituting acrylic scumble and artists' acrylic for the oil-based scumble and oil colours, and water for the linseed oil and white spirit. Apply the glaze and stipple as described opposite. Allow to dry (2–4 hours) and apply one coat of a matt or silk acrylic varnish as required. It is important to work quickly as water-based products dry faster than oil-based ones.

DRY BRUSHING

In this technique the brush is kept relatively dry as glaze is applied lightly over a base coat to create a cloudy effect. We have used a white base coat for all these examples, but the finish is just as successful on a tinted base or when the dry-brushed coat is the lighter. It can be subtle if applied in soft hues with soft strokes or bold if you use hard-bristled brushes and strong colours. An easy way to give texture to modern interiors, it is also used to create an aged finish for period settings – scene painters often use it to age scenery and props. It is ideal for highlighting architectural mouldings and, because it is extremely resilient, for furniture.

BASIC RECIPE – DEEP BLUE ON WHITE

INGREDIENTS

To cover approximately 12m² (129ft²)
Base coat ▶ 1 litre white vinyl matt emulsion
Glaze coat ▶ 250ml white vinyl matt emulsion / 250ml acrylic scumble glaze (transparent) / 3tbsp ultramarine artists' acrylic colour / 1tbsp neutral grey artists' acrylic colour / 125ml water
Optional protective coat ▶ 1 litre clear matt or silk acrylic varnish

EQUIPMENT

1 x 75mm (3in) decorators' brush or paint roller plus tray / container for mixing glaze / 1 x 50mm (2in) hard-bristled brush / scrap wooden board / 1 x 50mm (2in) varnish brush (optional)

INSTRUCTIONS
Base coat

Stir the emulsion well and apply an even coat to your prepared surface (see pp. 24–7) with the 75mm (3in) brush (or roller). Allow to dry (2–4 hours).

Glaze coat

1 Pour the emulsion into the container. Add the acrylic scumble, colours and water (a little at a time), stirring well.
2 Dip the tip of the hard-bristled brush into the glaze and remove excess paint on the wooden board. Working with random, short brush strokes, apply to the base. Recharge the brush as the glaze becomes too light, still letting some of the base show through. Leave to dry (2 hours).

Above left: This wall was dry brushed in several hues to give interest and variety. The dramatic mix of three separate glaze coats – green, lilac and purple applied in random patches and then blended together – has a modern feel that confirms an eclectic taste is at work here.

Notes For greater depth of colour, repeat the glazing stage once the paint is dry. For a hardwearing finish, apply one coat of varnish, according to the manufacturers' instructions.
Exterior use Substitute smooth masonry paint for the base coat and finish with two coats of polyurethane varnish.

❶ DEEP BLUE ON WHITE
The basic recipe colourway: this delightful bathroom blue was dry brushed only once.

❷ YELLOW ON WHITE
Here the bright glaze is tinted with 2tbsp cadmium yellow and ¹/₂tbsp vermilion red. This is a sunny, cheering scheme that would sit extremely well in the living or dining room of either a modern or more traditional home.

❸ PEACH PINK ON WHITE
The glaze colour is a mix of 2tbsp rose madder pink and 1tbsp titanium white, spiked with ¹/₂tsp cadmium yellow for a gentle, feminine look that would work in a bedroom.

❹ BRIGHT GREEN ON WHITE
This vibrant glaze is coloured with 2tbsp chromium green and 1tbsp cadmium yellow. The resulting tone would be ideal in a kitchen or bathroom. Try it in a garden room too, where it is surprisingly effective.

LOOSE-GLAZE BRUSHING

Loose-glaze brushing is a softer, looser form of dragging which we developed from period finishes we studied in stately homes of the eighteenth and early nineteenth centuries. Because the effect uses water-based paints it is simple to achieve and dries a great deal faster than conventional dragging (see p. 54) but to give much the same pleasing results. As the technique and materials require less effort to control than in oil-based dragging you can brush the glaze horizontally or diagonally as well as vertically, which makes it a versatile finish. A long-haired decorators' brush is the only tool you will need and this is far cheaper than a dragging brush. Another advantage of loose-glaze brushing is that it can be used on poor surfaces. The water-based glaze is thinner and the effect you are aiming for less precise, so minor imperfections tend not to show up. However, do fill any large cracks or holes to stop paint collecting there. As a resilient and hardwearing finish, loose-glaze brushing can also be used successfully on furniture.

This room has been loose-glaze brushed vertically in a soft green to give the same sense of height as vertical stripes. Although based upon period effects, the finish will adapt well to a variety of modern interiors.

BASIC RECIPE – DEEP GREEN ON MINT GREEN

INGREDIENTS

To cover approximately 12m² (129ft²)
Base coat ▶ 1 litre white vinyl matt emulsion / 2tbsp viridian green artists' acrylic colour / 1tbsp brilliant green artists' acrylic colour
Glaze coat ▶ 500ml white vinyl matt emulsion / 250ml acrylic scumble glaze (transparent) / 2tbsp viridian green artists' acrylic colour / 2tbsp oxide of chromium green artists' acrylic colour / 1tbsp emerald green artists' acrylic colour / 300ml water
Optional protective coat ▶ 1 litre clear matt or silk acrylic varnish

EQUIPMENT

2 containers / 1 x 75mm (3in) decorators' brush / 1 x 125mm (5in) long bristled decorators' brush / rags / 1 x 50mm (2in) varnish brush (optional)

INSTRUCTIONS

Base coat

1 Pour the emulsion into one of the containers. Add the viridian and brilliant greens and stir well.

2 Apply evenly to your prepared surface (see pp. 24–7) with the 75mm (3in) brush. Allow to dry (2–4 hours).

Glaze coat

1 Pour the emulsion into the other container. Add the acrylic scumble, viridian, oxide of chromium and emerald greens, and water (a little at a time), stirring well.

2 Load the 125mm (5in) brush with glaze and apply in a series of single, uninterrupted strokes, working from top to bottom of the surface and overlapping each stroke slightly.

3 Using the same brush, work over the surface again until faint brush lines appear on the glaze as you begin to drag it. Eradicate any drips with a rag. Allow to dry (2 hours).

Notes For a hardwearing finish, apply one coat of varnish, according to the manufacturers' instructions.

❶ DEEP GREEN ON MINT GREEN The basic, traditional colourway, but with diagonal brush strokes to suggest an engaging alternative. The effect is loose and free without being sloppy.

❷ STONE ON BLUE Here a pale glaze has been applied to a premixed deep blue emulsion base. The strokes are horizontal. The glaze colour-mix is 2tbsp titanium white, 1/2tbsp raw sienna and 1/2tbsp yellow ochre.

❸ PALE PINK ON RED This example, with vertical brushing, recalls the classic ragged look. The glaze is coloured with 2tbsp titanium white, 2tbsp cadmium red and 1/2tbsp rose madder pink and applied to a base of premixed deep red emulsion.

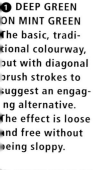

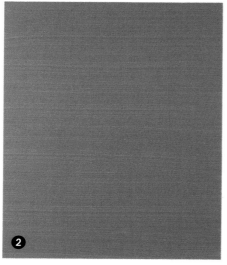

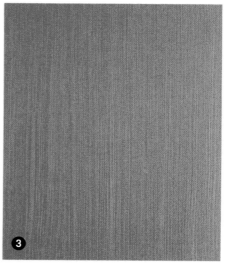

SIMPLE FRESCO

This finish gives the look often seen in old Italian frescos, where medieval painters perfected a technique which involved the application of water-based colours to wet plaster. Thankfully our recipe does not have to be applied to newly plastered walls – it just looks as if it does. Most authentic when undertaken in the colours of true fresco, this hardwearing effect is ideal for walls and ceilings and resilient enough for kitchens and bathrooms. A good way of ageing new interiors, it is also an excellent backdrop for stencilling. Plaster mouldings and other architectural details respond well to the technique too, and you can perform miracles with old furniture and frames.

BASIC RECIPE – TERRACOTTA ON CORAL

INGREDIENTS

To cover approximately 12m² (129ft²)
Base coat ▶ 1 litre white vinyl matt emulsion / 2tbsp venetian red artists' acrylic colour / ¹/₂tbsp raw sienna artists' acrylic colour
Glaze coat ▶ 500ml white vinyl matt emulsion / 250ml acrylic scumble glaze (transparent) / 2tbsp bronze ochre artists' acrylic colour / 2tbsp raw sienna artists' acrylic colour / ¹/₂tbsp venetian red artists' acrylic colour / 250ml water
Distressing the surface ▶ 1 x 500ml tin liming wax / 50g (1³/₄oz) whiting

EQUIPMENT

2 containers for mixing paint and glaze / 1 x 75mm (3in) decorators' brush / 1 x 50mm (2in) hard-bristled brush / disposable gloves / rags / water for soaking rags / medium-grade sandpaper

INSTRUCTIONS
Base coat

1 Pour the emulsion into one of the containers. Add the venetian red and raw sienna, and stir well.
2 Apply to the prepared surface (see pp. 24–7) with the decorators' brush, using random strokes. Allow to dry (2–4 hours).

Above left: Here the simple fresco technique has been applied to a plaster-cast head of Dante, using the archetypal terracotta on coral colourway of the basic recipe. Note how rubbing whiting into the surface has taken off some of the colour.

Glaze coat

1 Pour the emulsion into the other container. Add the acrylic scumble, bronze ochre, raw sienna, venetian red, and water (a little at a time), and stir well.
2 Apply to the base coat, using the hard-bristled brush. Work in all directions, using rough, uneven brush strokes.
3 Wear gloves for all the remaining stages. Quickly immerse a rag in water and wring it out until almost dry. Use the damp rag to rub the glaze into the base coat with a circular motion, varying the effect as much as possible. Allow to dry (1 hour).

Distressing the surface

1 Rub sandpaper over the surface in some areas to remove some of the paint.

2 Rub liming wax into other areas on a clean rag.

3 Again using a clean rag, quickly rub a little whiting into the waxed areas to create a dusty effect.

Notes If you want a greater depth of colour, repeat the glazing and sandpapering sequences before you begin steps 2–3 of Distressing the surface.

Exterior use Substitute smooth masonry paint in the base coat and finish with two coats of matt polyurethane varnish.

❶ TERRACOTTA ON CORAL
On a flat surface the basic colourway seems to gain intensity. This is a rich scheme for a grand neoclassical living room.

❷ COBALT BLUE ON STONE
The base coat is tinted with 1tbsp raw sienna and 1tbsp burnt umber, and the glaze with 3tbsp cobalt blue and 1tbsp prussian blue for a colour popular in medieval frescos.

❸ GREEN ON STONE
This bright variation is an experiment in modern colours. The base coat is made as for sample 2, while the glaze colour-mix is 3tbsp bright green with 1tbsp yellow ochre.

❹ SALMON PINK ON STONE
Another fresco scheme, this would suit modern or period rooms. The stone base of sample 2 softens a glaze tinted with 2tbsp rose madder pink, 1/2tbsp titanium white and 1/2tsp yellow ochre.

MOCK PLASTER

This *faux* finish, with its look of aged paint brushed onto rough plaster, was reputedly first used in French café-bars of the 1970s. In fact, the broken-colour effect requires a conventional emulsion base, topped with a mix of whiting and powder pigment rubbed into a layer of wax. You can adapt this recipe to use subtle earth hues, but experimenting with bright colours is fun and the real delight of working with pigment is the intensity of colour you can achieve. Remember, though, that the strength of pigment colour can be alarming on first view so run several tests before you begin painting. Pigment colours also need to be thoroughly mixed; if you decide to tone them down by adding more whiting, make sure you avoid streaking.

A mock-plaster finish can add interest to plaster mouldings and other architectural details. We used cadmium green to highlight a standard ceiling rose.

The finish works best on a white base but tints can be used successfully: remember you must use acrylic artists' colour with the water-based emulsion. Mock plaster will suit new or old interiors, and the waxed surface makes it easy to wipe clean. Try it on garden ornaments too, especially those made of plaster.

BASIC RECIPE – ULTRAMARINE ON WHITE

INGREDIENTS
To cover approximately 12m² (129ft²)
Base coats ▶ 2 litres white vinyl matt emulsion
Top coat ▶ 1 x 500ml tub white wax / 250g (8³/₄oz) ultramarine powder pigment / 250g (8³/₄oz) whiting or chalk powder

EQUIPMENT
1 x 75mm (3in) decorators' brush or paint roller plus tray / rags protective mask / small container for mixing pigment / 1 x 50mm (2in) varnish brush (optional)

INSTRUCTIONS
Base coats
Stir the emulsion well and apply two even coats to your prepared surface (see pp. 24–7), using the brush (or roller). Allow 2–4 hours for each coat to dry.

Topcoat
1 Using a rag and a circular action, rub a thick but even layer of white wax into the base coat.
2 Put on the mask. Place the ultramarine and whiting (or chalk powder) in the container and stir well.
3 Using another rag, rub the whiting mixture quickly into the wax with a downward action to give a broken colour finish very like real plaster. Allow to dry completely (2–3 hours).

Notes Repeat the topcoat with a toning colour (see pp. 30–31) to vary the effect.
Exterior use Add a coat of wax polish after the topcoat to protect the surface of your piece.

❶ ULTRAMARINE ON WHITE
The basic recipe: this strong colour is ideal for a bathroom, where mock plaster's wipe-clean qualities would be appreciated.

❷ PINK ON WHITE
Three powder pigments are used to create a dramatic pink for the topcoat: 125g (4²/₅oz) alizarin crimson and 100g (3¹/₂oz) magenta, sharpened with 25g (⁹/₁₀ oz) ultramarine. Follow the basic recipe for the base coats.

❸ OCHRE ON WHITE
A sample to demonstrate the use of pure yellow ochre pigment in the topcoat (quantity as for the basic recipe). This stunning variation would look delightful in a traditional interior. Again, follow the basic recipe for the base coats.

RUBBED-BACK PLASTER

This technique is inspired by the rough-painted walls in unrestored artisan cottages of the late nineteenth and early twentieth centuries. Money and time were limited so the inhabitants often painted straight over the previous colour in a single coat, making the paint stretch further by applying it sparingly or by diluting it with water. The effect is achieved by adding whiting to contrasting glazes to age them, by applying the paint roughly with hard-bristled brushes and by rubbing down with sandpaper. The result is similar, but softer, than limewashing.

BASIC RECIPE – AQUAMARINE ON PALE PINK

INGREDIENTS

To cover approximately 12m² (129ft²)
Base coat ▶ 1 litre white vinyl matt emulsion
First colour ▶ 250ml white vinyl matt emulsion / 125ml rose madder pink artists' acrylic colour / 100g (3¹/₂oz) whiting / 125ml water
Second colour ▶ 250ml white vinyl matt emulsion / 4tbsp turquoise blue artists' acrylic colour / 2tbsp bright green artists' acrylic colour / 1tbsp cobalt blue artists' acrylic colour / 100g (3¹/₂oz) whiting / 125ml water
Optional protective coat ▶ 1 litre clear matt acrylic varnish

EQUIPMENT

1 x 75mm (3in) decorators' brush or paint roller plus tray / 2 containers for mixing colours / 2 x 75mm (3in) hard-bristled brushes / disposable gloves / medium-grade sandpaper / 1 x 50mm (2in) varnish brush (optional)

INSTRUCTIONS
Base coat

Stir the emulsion well and apply an even coat to your prepared surface (see pp. 24–7), using the 75mm (3in) decorators' brush (or roller). Allow to dry (2–4 hours).

First colour

1 Pour the emulsion into one of the containers and add rose madder pink, whiting and water (a little at a time), stirring well.
2 Using one of the hard-bristled brushes, apply to the base coat in random strokes. Allow to dry (2–3 hours).
3 Put on the gloves and rub sandpaper gently over the surface to reveal some of the base coat.

Second colour

1 Pour the emulsion into the other container. Add the turquoise, green, cobalt blue and whiting (or chalk powder), and mix. Then add the water (a little at a time), stirring well.
2 Using the other hard-bristled brush, apply to the first colour in random strokes. Allow to dry (2–3 hours).
3 Sand vigorously to reveal some of the first colour and base.

Notes For a hardwearing finish, apply one coat of varnish, according to the manufacturers' instructions.
Exterior use Substitute smooth masonry paint for the base coat and finish with two coats of matt polyurethane varnish.

❶ AQUAMARINE ON PALE PINK
The basic recipe: this subtle finish has a cloudy, aged look which is extremely appealing. The colourway would suit a bath-room or bedroom.

❷ PALE GREEN ON OLIVE
The first colour here is a deep, pre-mixed olive green, and the top colour simply 250ml white vinyl matt emulsion, tinted with 1tbsp viridian green. Follow the basic recipe for quantities of whiting and water.

❸ CREAMY WHITE ON YELLOW
A bright scheme for a kitchen, living or dining room: 2tbsp cadmium yellow is used to tint the first colour coat, with a dash (1/2tbsp) of raw umber for the topcoat.

❹ WARM GREY ON WHITE
This gentle colour-way could be used in modern or period homes. The first colour coat is pure white, while the second is tinted with 2tbsp neutral grey and 1/2tbsp yellow ochre.

TEXTURING

There are many different ways to texture paint. You can add sawdust for a coarse grain or whiting for subtlety – here we use fine sand in the base coat for a medium-grade finish. The way you apply your mix can give surface interest too. The obvious advantage of texturing is that it is a wonderful disguise for imperfect walls. But it can bring character to any surface, or a tough finish to a garden room or exterior wall. Premixed textured paints are now available in a wider colour range, although in most cases it is more satisfactory to mix your own using artists' acrylics, and the brighter hues make this simple technique remarkably versatile. The samples here use a white base as it best illustrates the finish. But the emulsion can be tinted before sand is added. Try texturing garden ornaments: statues and pots take on an antique look when a textured base is used under a rust, verdigris or lead finish (see pp.106–11).

Textured finishes inside and out: a bold, contemporary use of colour and surface interest have combined to make this an excellent choice for a minimalist home in Mexico.

BASIC RECIPE – YELLOW OCHRE ON WHITE

INGREDIENTS

To cover approximately 12m² (129ft²)
Base coat ▸ 1 litre white vinyl matt emulsion / 250g (8³/₄oz) fine sand
Glaze coat ▸ 250ml white vinyl matt emulsion / 250ml acrylic scumble glaze /
artists' acrylic colours: 2tbsp yellow ochre and 1tbsp raw sienna / 150ml water
Optional protective coat ▸ 1 litre clear matt acrylic varnish

EQUIPMENT

2 containers for mixing paint and glaze / 2 x 75mm (3in) decorators'
brushes / 1 x 50mm (2in) varnish brush (optional)

❶ YELLOW OCHRE ON WHITE
The basic recipe colourway, demonstrating two different textures above and below a dado rail colourwashed (see p. 48) in purple. More sand (360g or 12³/₄oz) was added to the base coat used on the lower panel to create a distinctly heavier texture.

❷ SOFT GREY ON WHITE
This sample illustrates the potential subtlety of the finish. A little very fine sand (115g or 4oz) was used in the base coat to create the gentle texturing, and 2tbsp neutral grey and ¹/₂tbsp magenta coloured the glaze.

❸ ROSE ON WHITE
A strong colour for a modern interior: the glaze is tinted with 3tbsp magenta and 1tbsp cadmium red, mellowed with ¹/₂tbsp burnt umber. Again 360g (12³/₄oz) sand was added to the base coat.

INSTRUCTIONS

Base coat

Pour the emulsion into a container. Add the sand, stirring well. Apply to the prepared surface (see pp. 24–7). Allow to dry (2–4 hours).

Glaze coat

1 Pour the emulsion into the other container. Add the acrylic scumble, yellow ochre, raw sienna, and water (a little at a time) and stir well.

2 Apply to the base coat in random brush strokes. Work over the glaze several times, still allowing some of the base coat to show through. Leave to dry (2–3 hours).

Notes For a hardwearing finish, apply one coat of varnish.
Exterior use Use textured masonry paint for the base coat (no sand needed) and finish with matt polyurethane varnish.

AGEING WOOD

Wood ages naturally through general wear and tear. Furniture exposed to sunlight fades, and polished wood slowly darkens as it collects dust and grime. It is that sense of time past that gives any well-used and loved piece its appeal, and since the nineteenth century craftsmen have striven to simulate this look on new wood. Virtually any wood can be aged, and there are any number of reasons for wanting to do so. Perhaps you have a new pine chest that needs to be aged to fit alongside older pieces. Or maybe a move to a more traditional home has left modern pieces looking out of place. The distressing techniques may seem a little drastic, but it is down to you to decide how far to go.

BASIC RECIPE – AGEING PINE

INGREDIENTS

For a small wooden chest
Antiquing glaze ▶ 500ml PVA adhesive or white glue / 1 litre water / 40g (1²/₅oz) raw sienna powder pigment / 40g (1²/₅oz) raw umber powder pigment (one coat)
Optional protective coat ▶ 500ml clear matt acrylic varnish (one coat)

EQUIPMENT

Bradawl or 50mm (2in) nail and hammer / craft knife (optional) / container for mixing glaze / 1 x 75mm (3in) paint brush / lint-free cotton rags / 1 x 50mm (2in) varnish brush (optional)

This modern pine chest has been aged with a glaze that suggests something of the look of liming. You can still see the original colour – just inside the open drawer. The PVA adhesive solution was coloured with 40g (1²/₅ oz) burnt umber and 30g (1oz) white powder pigment. The modern knobs were replaced with others more in keeping with its aged look.

INSTRUCTIONS
Distressing the wood

Use the bradawl (or nail and hammer) to make the small clusters of holes typical of woodworm. You can also, if you like, add occasional scratches, using a craft knife, and small indentations with the hammer.

Antiquing glaze

1 Pour the PVA adhesive (or white glue) into the container. Add the water (a little at a time) and stir well.
2 Add the raw sienna and raw umber and again stir well, making sure that no lumps remain.
3 Brush the glaze onto your prepared surface (see pp. 24–7) in random strokes.
4 Make a flat pad of cotton rag and use it to rub the glaze into the surface, paying particular attention to the distressed areas. (This process will also help remove any excess glaze.) Change the rag frequently as it will quickly become clogged with glaze. On small areas the drying time is approx. 1 hour; if you are ageing a large surface, such as a floor, work on an area no larger than 2m² (6ft²) at a time.

Notes Repeat the glaze stage for a greater depth of colour. For a more hardwearing finish apply one or two coats of varnish, following the manufacturers' instructions.

❶ AGEING PINE
Here the basic recipe colourway is applied to a new pine drawer. The resulting dark colour represents the look pine wood might acquire after some years in a hardworking area such as a kitchen.

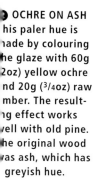

❷ OCHRE ON ASH
This paler hue is made by colouring the glaze with 60g (2oz) yellow ochre and 20g (³/₄oz) raw umber. The resulting effect works well with old pine. The original wood was ash, which has a greyish hue.

❸ GREY ON LIMED WOOD
Two antiquing glazes are used to create a grey tone on limed wood. The first glaze is tinted with 30g (1oz) white and 20g (³/₄oz) black, while the second one is coloured with 20g (³/₄oz) burnt umber and 10g (¹/₃oz) ultramarine blue.

WATER-BASED CRACKLE

The simulation of the crazing that appears on painted or varnished furniture when the underlying wood expands and contracts as a result of changes in temperature was first undertaken in France as early as the eighteenth century. Today, with the help of proprietary preparations, this ageing technique seems almost magical in its simplicity. One or two coats of a transparent crackle varnish (or craquelure) are applied over a coloured base coat which has been allowed to dry. As the crackle varnish itself dries, it begins to work against the base coat and cracks appear in its surface. Then, when the contrasting topcoat is applied and left to dry, the base-coat colour is thrown into relief and the cracks become even more apparent. Tinted glazes can also be rubbed into the surface to enhance and antique the finish. The effect is traditional or contemporary, depending on the colour combination you choose. A natural for wood and plaster – it captures something of the ageing often seen on Italian Renaissance frescos and painted panels – crackle can also translate even the ugliest plastic laminate into a new dimension.

BASIC RECIPE – STONE ON BLUE

INGREDIENTS

To cover approximately 6m² (65ft²)
Base coat ▶ 500ml premixed sky blue vinyl matt emulsion
Crackle coat ▶ 250ml acrylic crackle varnish (transparent)
Topcoat ▶ 500ml premixed stone emulsion
Optional antiquing coat ▶ 250ml pale antiquing patina
Protective coat ▶ 500ml clear satin acrylic varnish (one coat)

EQUIPMENT

2 x 50mm (2in) decorators' brushes / 1 x 25mm (1in) paint brush / 1 x 50mm (2in) varnish brush / rags (optional)

INSTRUCTIONS

Base coat

Stir the emulsion well and apply one coat to your prepared surface (pp. 24–7), using one of the decorators' brushes. Allow to dry (2–4 hours). A premixed emulsion reacts more effectively against the crackle varnish so don't mix a colour.

Crackle coat

Using the paint brush, apply one coat of crackle varnish to the entire surface, working horizontally if you want horizontal cracks and vertically if you want vertical ones. As it dries, the varnish begins to crack or craze. The thicker this coat is the fewer and larger the cracks will be; the more it is worked the finer and more numerous. Allow to dry (2 hours).

Above left: The horizontal crazing on this simple MDF box was created by brushing a single coat of water-based crackle varnish in one direction over a base of premixed stone emulsion. The topcoat is a premixed deep blue emulsion.

WATER-BASED CRACKLE

❶ STONE ON BLUE
The basic colourway: two coats of crackle varnish are applied in opposite directions for an attractive, heavily crazed effect. The final two coats of protective varnish will make this an extremely durable surface.

❷ PEA ON STRAW
Two coats of crackle varnish, again cross brushed, over a base coat of straw-coloured emulsion: the pea green of the topcoat was widely used in Victorian times so this scheme would suit a nineteenth-century interior.

❸ SOFT LILAC ON ICECREAM YELLOW
This colourway works well in a modern setting. Here again two coats of cross-brushed crackle varnish are used.

❹ DEEP RED ON STONE
For a colour combination popular in the Victorian era: a stone emulsion base coat under a deep red topcoat. Only one coat of crackle was applied in vertical strokes.

❺ WARM GREY ON BRICK
The deep red base under warm grey is typical of the Georgian period, and the two coats of crackle varnish are cross brushed and well worked to create fine crazing.

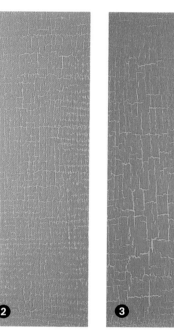

WATER-BASED CRACKLE

Topcoat
Stir the emulsion well, brush an even coat onto the crazed surface using the other decorators' brush, and leave to dry (2–4 hours). As the topcoat dries, the cracks will become apparent once more, revealing the blue of the base coat. (You can speed the drying process with a hairdryer.)

The palest green water-based crackle on a panelled wall could work wonderfully well in a period setting.

Protective coat
Using the varnish brush, apply one coat of varnish, according to the manufacturers' instructions. Repeat if a particularly hardwearing finish is required.

Notes If you want an even more pronounced effect, repeat the crackle stage before applying the topcoat, brushing the varnish on in the opposite direction. For a more antique finish, use a rag to rub in a layer of antiquing patina after the topcoat has dried and leave to dry (1 hour) before applying the protective coat.

OIL-BASED CRACKLE

Oil-based crackle produces an effect of greater age than its water-based counterpart (see p. 74) and cracks tend to be more widely spaced and varied. Here two layers of transparent crackle varnish are standard, and they work against each other while drying. A tinted glaze brushed on and rubbed off to remain only in the cracks completes the effect. The look can be subtle or bold, depending on the colour contrast. Oil-based crackle varnish is an unpredictable material. Experience has taught us three things: follow the manufacturers' instructions, use premixed paint for the base coat, and work in an evenly heated, dry area. It is also best confined to small, flat surfaces. But do not be put off. Crackle is a remarkable finish that can produce wonderful results.

BASIC RECIPE – RED ON BLACK

INGREDIENTS

To cover approximately 7m² (75ft²)
Base coat ▶ 500ml premixed black gloss paint
Crackle coats ▶ 1 litre premixed oil-based crackle varnish (transparent)
Topcoat ▶ 2tbsp cadmium red artists' oil colour / 1tbsp oil-based scumble glaze / 1tbsp white spirit
Optional protective coats ▶ 1 litre clear satin or gloss polyurethane varnish

EQUIPMENT

2–3 x 50mm (2in) paint brushes / 1 x 25mm (1in) varnish brush / container for mixing glaze / rags

INSTRUCTIONS

Base coat

ALWAYS WORK IN A WELL-VENTILATED AREA

Stir the gloss paint thoroughly and use one of the paint brushes to apply two even coats to your prepared surface (see pp. 24–7), allowing 24 hours for each coat to dry.

Crackle coats

1 Apply an even coat of crackle varnish to the surface, using the varnish brush, and leave until tacky (approx. 30 minutes).
2 Brush on a second coat and allow both coats to dry completely (1 hour). As the second coat dries, it pulls against the first, creating fine cracks in the surface of the varnish.

Two variations on the basic recipe: (left) a dark green gloss base coat and a topcoat tinted with 2tbsp jaune brillant; (right) a deep red gloss base coat and a topcoat colour-mix of 1tbsp titanium white, ¹/₂tbsp cadmium red and ¹/₂tbsp jaune brillant.

OIL-BASED CRACKLE

❶ RED ON BLACK
The classic colour-way of the basic recipe: a striking combination which works well with Chinese antiques.

❷ BLUE ON OCHRE
This modern look can find a place in a traditional home. A deep antique yellow is used for the gloss base coat, and the topcoat is coloured with 2½tbsp cobalt blue and ½tbsp titanium white.

❸ RED ON ANTIQUE YELLOW
An authentic look: cracks in the stone gloss base coat are revealed with a topcoat colour-mix of 1tbsp yellow ochre, ½tbsp red oxide and ½tbsp raw umber.

❹ PALE GREY ON BURGUNDY
Another bold colourway in the oriental style. The crazing over the burgundy gloss base coat is tinted with a topcoat coloured with 1tbsp neutral grey and 1tbsp titanium white.

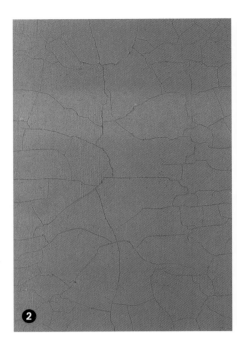

Topcoat

1 Place the cadmium red in the container. Add the oil-based scumble and white spirit and stir well.

2 Apply an even coat to the entire surface, using a second paint brush.

3 Wipe most of the glaze off with clean rags – when you have finished, red glaze should remain only in the cracks. It is important to keep changing rags or you will begin recoating the surface with glaze. Allow to dry (24 hours).

Notes For a more hardwearing finish, apply two coats of varnish with a third paint brush, following the manufacturers' instructions.

RUBBING OFF ON WOOD

We developed this technique to colour and age wood simultaneously in a subtle and stylish way. It is an immensely satisfying method of giving old wood a new lease of life and an equally effective route to creating furniture that blends with your decor. Searching junk shops for old pieces to transform is fun – simple, uncluttered lines are often the most successful. The effect is soft, as some of the wood's colour remains visible, and the detail and graining are still apparent, but dark varnish works against it so have wood stripped if necessary before sealing it. If you decide to work with a new or immaculate piece, you can opt to age it first, and, of course, there is no need to limit yourself to one colour. You could choose one for the legs and back of a chair and another for the seat. Seal the entire surface and use masking tape (removing most of the tackiness on a cloth) to protect areas you do not want to colour with your first glaze. Then apply and rub off as in the recipe; remask and follow the same process for your second colour.

BASIC RECIPE – MOSS GREEN ON BLOND WOOD

INGREDIENTS

To cover approximately 6m² (65ft²)
Sealant coat ▶ 1 x 500ml white polish
Rubbed-off glaze ▶ 500ml white vinyl matt emulsion / 2tbsp acrylic scumble glaze (transparent) / 1tbsp hooker's green artists' acrylic colour / ¹/₂tbsp pale olive green artists' acrylic colour / ¹/₂tbsp yellow ochre artists' acrylic colour / 1tbsp water (one coat)
Optional protective coat ▶ 500ml clear matt or satin acrylic varnish

EQUIPMENT

Bradawl or 50mm (2in) nail and hammer (optional) / craft knife (optional) / lint-free cloths / medium-grade sandpaper / container for mixing glaze / 1 x 50mm (2in) paint brush / 1 x 50mm (2in) varnish brush (optional)

INSTRUCTIONS

Ageing (optional)

Use the bradawl (or 50mm/2in nail and hammer) to make the small clusters of holes typical of woodworm in your prepared surface. You can also add occasional scratches, using a craft knife, and small indentations with a hammer.

Sealant coat

1 Form a pad of lint-free cloth and apply a thin, even coat of white polish. Allow to dry (1 hour) and buff with a clean cloth.
2 Using the sandpaper, rub lightly over the entire surface. Your aim is to create a slightly rougher surface to which the glaze coat will adhere, but it is important that you do not take off too much of the polish.

Above and p. 80: These chairs were stripped and left to dry for 7 days before work began. Colours as follows. Green: basic recipe. Lilac: 1¹/₂tbsp pale violet and ¹/₂tbsp titanium white. Blue: 1¹/₂tbsp ultramarine and ¹/₂tbsp burnt umber. Sand: 1¹/₂tbsp yellow ochre and ¹/₂tbsp raw umber.

❶ MOSS GREEN ON BLOND WOOD The colours of the basic recipe give a natural look for a country home. A durable, hardwearing finish, it would do especially well in the kitchen. In all four examples, rubbing off in the direction of the grain has produced an effect almost like dragging.

❷ RICH UMBER A versatile colourway that brings a natural, deep tone to the wood: 2tbsp raw umber colour the glaze mix.

❸ VIOLET This contemporary look is created by tinting the glaze with 2tbsp brilliant purple.

❹ TURQUOISE Another bright, modern look, its seaside tones would be fun in a bathroom. The glaze is coloured with 1^1/2tbsp turquoise blue and ^{1}/2tbsp cobalt blue.

Rubbed-off glaze

1 Pour the emulsion into the container. Add the acrylic scumble, hooker's and pale olive greens, yellow ochre, and water (a little at a time), stirring well.

2 Apply the glaze thickly onto the entire surface with the paint brush and leave until it becomes tacky (approx. 5 minutes).

3 Using another cloth, wipe most of the glaze off – your aim is to leave a fine haze of colour on the flat surfaces and a build-up of glaze in any detail. Allow to dry (2 hours).

Notes Repeat the rubbing off stage if you want a greater depth of colour. For a more hardwearing finish, apply a coat of varnish, according to the manufacturers' instructions.

Exterior use Finish with two coats of satin polyurethane varnish, again according to the manufacturers' instructions.

WOODWASHING

This simple way to colour wood creates a pale, washed effect. It is ideal for kitchens and for pieces of furniture that you wish to fit into a new scheme or setting. Like the previous finish but even easier to handle, the look is soft, with the graining and detail of the wood still visible. It is also an ideal way to improve the cheaper soft woods, making them an attractive option for the budget conscious. Premixed wood washes are now available but the colour range is limited and mixing your own is cheaper. Varnish surfaces you plan to use in kitchen and bathroom.

❶ DEEP BLUE
The basic recipe: this subtle look, showing plenty of the wood's graining through the glaze, would work well in a kitchen or bathroom.

❷ DUSKY PINK
Another soft colourway with the beauty of the wood still apparent: 1tbsp alizarin crimson, 1tbsp titanium white, ¹/₂tbsp raw sienna and ¹/₂tbsp lilac make the delicate tones.

❸ PALE GREEN
A subtle colour, versatile in kitchens and conservatories, it was created by colouring the wash with 2tbsp sap green, 1tbsp raw sienna and ¹/₂tbsp titanium white.

❹ RAW SIENNA
A versatile colour to enhance most new woods: the colour-mix is 2tbsp raw sienna and 1tbsp raw umber.

BASIC RECIPE – DEEP BLUE

INGREDIENTS

To cover approximately 6m² (65ft²)
500ml white vinyl matt emulsion / 2tbsp ultramarine artists' acrylic colour / 1tbsp cobalt blue artists' acrylic colour / ¹/₂tbsp burnt umber artists' acrylic colour / 150–200ml water
Optional protective coat ▶ 500ml matt or satin acrylic varnish (one coat)

EQUIPMENT

Container for mixing wash coat / 1 x 75mm (3in) decorators' brush / lint-free cloth / 1 x 50mm (2in) varnish brush (optional)

INSTRUCTIONS

1 Pour the emulsion into the container. Add the ultramarine, cobalt blue, burnt umber, and water (a little at a time), stirring continuously – you are aiming for a milky consistency.
2 Using the decorators' brush, apply the wash to the wood, working always in the direction of the grain – you should be able to see it through the thin wash. Allow to dry a little (15–20 minutes).
3 Make a pad with a lint-free cloth and wipe the surface to reveal further grain and texture. Leave to dry (1 hour).

Notes If you want a hardwearing finish, seal with one or two coats of varnish, according to the manufacturers' instructions.

Above: Door and skirting board have been woodwashed in a lovely blue. This is an ideal finish to complement the stained-plaster look of the walls.

AGEING PAINT

We devised this effective technique to give furniture and fittings the appearance of many layers of paint slowly peeling off after decades of wear and tear. The art of simulating ageing paint, like crackle (see pp. 74–8), dates back to eighteenth-century France, and it is still an excellent way to make cheaper, new wood look as though it has been in your home for years. The finish can have a period look, through the use of dark reds and greens, or a more contemporary one, with bright, contrasting hues; and peeling can be subtle or emphatic, depending on the degree of ageing. To create an authentic look, study genuine old pieces before you begin and discover where natural ageing occurs.

BASIC RECIPE – DEEP YELLOW ON BURNT UMBER

INGREDIENTS

To cover approximately 6m² (65ft²)

Wax coat ▶ 1 x 250ml tin furniture wax (clear) or beeswax

Wash coat ▶ 2tbsp burnt umber artists' acrylic colour / 1tbsp water

Emulsion coat ▶ 500ml white vinyl matt emulsion / 2tbsp cadmium yellow artists' acrylic colour / 1tbsp bronze ochre artists' acrylic colour / 1/2tbsp venetian red artists' acrylic colour

Glaze coat ▶ 500ml white vinyl matt emulsion / 1tbsp cadmium yellow artists' acrylic colour / 1/2tbsp bronze ochre artists' acrylic colour / 4tbsp water

Optional protective coat ▶ 250ml furniture polish (clear) or 500ml clear satin acrylic varnish

EQUIPMENT

1 x 25mm (1in) paint brush / pencil / paper (for sketch plan) / 3 containers for mixing wash, emulsion and glaze / 1 x 25mm (1in) decorators' brush / 2 x 50mm (2in) decorators' brushes / scraper or spatula / rags / medium-grade sandpaper / 1 x 50mm (2in) varnish brush (optional)

INSTRUCTIONS

Wax coat

Using the paint brush, dab wax onto those areas of the prepared wooden surface (see pp. 24–7) you wish to reveal. It is best to apply the wax evenly in a series of lines rather than random strokes, but vary the size and spacing as much as possible. This is essentially a resist technique – paint will not adhere permanently to the waxed areas – so you must visualize the final effect and sketch it as a reminder when you begin to distress the paint later. Leave to dry (24 hours).

Wash coat

1 Place the burnt umber in one of the containers and add the water (a little at a time), stirring well.
2 Use the 25mm (1in) decorators' brush to apply the wash to the wood in the direction of the grain. Allow to dry (1 hour).

Emulsion coat

1 Pour the emulsion into a second container. Add the cadmium yellow, bronze ochre and venetian red and stir well.

Opposite: This new occasional table was aged using a shortened version of the ageing paint technique. The bright yellow was created by using 3tbsp cadmium yellow in the wash, the emulsion coat was omitted, and the glaze was coloured with 2tbsp bright green.

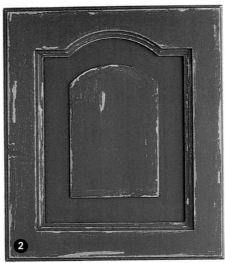

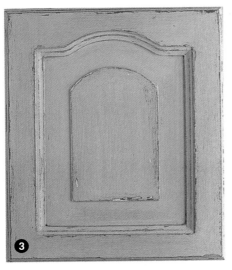

❶ DEEP YELLOW ON BURNT UMBER The basic recipe: this natural mix is typical of French country furniture and would be good in a kitchen, where it makes a hard-wearing finish.

❷ BURGUNDY ON CORAL There is a country feel to this rich colourway too, another variation on the basic recipe Here a wash coat is not used. The emulsion coat is tinted with 2tbsp cadmium red, 1/2tbsp titanium white and 1/2tbsp raw sienna. The glaze-coat mix use 2tbsp raw sienna and 1tbsp red oxide

❸ PALE BLUE ON ULTRAMARINE Again the wash coat is omitted. The emulsion coat is coloured with 3tbsp ultramarine blue, and the glaze with 1tbsp cobalt blue, 1tbsp light ultra-marine blue and 1tbsp titanium white.

❹ PURPLE ON STONE This contemporary version tints the wash coat with 50g (1 3/4oz) yellow ochre powder pigment. The other coats revert to acrylic colour: for the emulsion, 3tbsp yellow ochre; for the glaze, 2tbsp brilliant purple an 1tbsp cobalt blue.

2 Using one of the 50mm (2in) decorators' brushes, apply an even coat of paint to the surface in the direction of the grain. Allow to dry (2–4 hours).

Glaze coat

1 Pour the emulsion into a third container. Add the cadmium yellow, bronze ochre, and water (gradually), stirring well.

2 Apply an even coat in the direction of the grain, using the other 50mm (2in) decorators' brush. Allow to dry a little (30–40 minutes).

Distressing the paint

1 Referring to your sketch plan, use the scraper (or spatula) and rags to remove as many layers of paint as you can in the waxed areas.

2 Smooth the rough edges of the paint with sandpaper.

Notes If you want a more hardwearing finish, seal the surface with a layer of furniture polish or with a coat of varnish, according to the manufacturers' instructions.

This door has been painted in colours typical of the Scandinavian palette, using an ageing paint technique (see p. 85), and the wall painting is a characteristic floral design.

In recent years the Scandinavian colour palette has become increasingly popular. It is a look that derives largely from nature. The misty, cool blues and greens of those northern landscapes predominate, spiked with a variety of earth tones in the highly decorated detailing of plants and flowers. It was in the long winter months, when the elements prevented work on the land, that peasant men and women spent many hours carving and painting the cupboards, dressers and chests that are now so much admired. A characteristic simplicity of form and airy lightness of effect make this an ideal look for kitchens and bathrooms.

In this recipe we have devised a simple, undecorated, aged finish which works well with the Scandinavian colour palette. As a broken-colour technique – that is, as a glaze applied on a contrasting flat base coat and then rubbed back – it has authenticity, as well as plenty of texture and body. It is ideal for furniture that receives heavy wear and, because it uses water-based products, is easy to apply to most wooden surfaces. This is a charming way of rejuvenating old kitchen cupboards.

BASIC RECIPE – BLUE-GREY ON IVY GREEN

INGREDIENTS

To cover approximately 6m² (65ft²)

Emulsion coat ▶ 500ml white vinyl matt emulsion / 3tbsp hooker's green artists' acrylic colour / 2tbsp pale olive green artists' acrylic colour

Glaze coat ▶ 500ml white vinyl matt emulsion / 3tbsp monestial blue artists' acrylic colour / 1tbsp cobalt blue artists' acrylic colour / 1tbsp payne's grey artists' acrylic colour / 2tbsp water (one coat)

Optional protective coat ▶ 500ml clear satin acrylic varnish

EQUIPMENT

2 containers for mixing paint / 2 x 50mm (2in) decorators' brushes / rags / 1 x 50mm (2in) varnish brush (optional)

INSTRUCTIONS

Emulsion coat

1 Pour the emulsion into one of the containers. Add the hooker's and pale olive greens and stir well.

2 Apply to your prepared surface (see pp. 24–7), working in the direction of the grain, and allow to dry (2–4 hours).

Glaze coat

1 Pour the emulsion into the other container. Add the monestial blue, cobalt blue, payne's grey, and water (a little at a time), stirring well.

2 Apply to the entire surface in the direction of the grain.

3 When this coat is set but not dry (approx. 30 minutes), wipe off gently with a rag, working again in the direction of the grain to reveal some of the emulsion coat. Allow to dry (2–3 hours).

Notes For a deeper tone, repeat the glaze coat or leave the water out of that stage. If you decide to use no water, the glaze will dry more quickly so do not wait for it to set before

❶ BLUE-GREY ON IVY GREEN
The classic tones and an ideal base for decoration: the glaze coat was left to set for approx. 10 minutes.

❷ GREEN ON STONE
This is made by colouring the emulsion coat with 2tbsp yellow ochre, and the glaze with 3tbsp forest green and 1tbsp monestial green.

❸ GREY ON PALE BLUE
The emulsion coat is tinted with 3tbsp cobalt blue, and the glaze with 3tbsp neutral grey and 2tbsp burnt umber.

❹ CORAL ON UMBER
A modern alternative: colour the emulsion coat with 4tbsp burnt umber, the glaze with 2tbsp raw sienna.

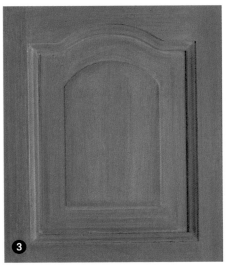

wiping off. If you want a more hardwearing finish, apply one coat of varnish, according to the manufacturers' instructions. **Exterior use** It is best to follow Scandinavian custom and use wood staining for exterior surfaces. Oil-based and water-based wood stains are available in a range of colours. Finish with a polyurethane varnish, following the manufacturers' instructions: satin is better for looks, but gloss will last longer. For exterior woodwork, such as window frames and shutters, oil-based stains can be used, but again remember to finish with polyurethane varnish for durability.

The trompe l'oeil windows contribute to this unusually flamboyant Scandinavian interior. Much more traditional in feel are the handsome panelling and beautifully decorated chair backs.

SHAKER

The Shaker look seems to speak to many people today. Perhaps it is the simplicity and sheer coherence of the Shaker way of life that appeals. Every aspect of Shaker life was organized and this is reflected in their simple architecture, home decoration and furnishing.

They painted the exteriors of their work buildings in tans and yellows, more expensive white paint was restricted to meeting houses. Their homes were often painted cream, with dark brown, bottle green or deep red woodwork inside. The believers liked bold, solid colours and although their furnishings were characteristically free of ornamentation, the shapes and colours are extremely attractive.

In their frugal, self-supporting communities paint was often hard to come by and had to be made from available materials. Whole milk was the usual medium, mixed with costly powder pigments and a little lime and the resulting milk (or casein paints were cheap, durable and easy to apply, drying to a flat smooth finish with a depth of colour seldom found in synthetic paints. Milk paints can still be bought today, in a wide range of Shaker colours, although now they are sold either premixed with buttermilk or skimmed-milk powders or simply as pigment with instructions for mixing. They are certainly the best way of creating the authentic colours of a Shaker home: We recommend that you use them for this recipe, which depends for its aged effect on an extremely simple resist technique.

This deep brown panelling is typical of Shaker colouring. Their unpainted woods were often maple and pine.

BASIC RECIPE – DEEP COLONIAL RED ON YELLOW OCHRE

INGREDIENTS	**To cover approximately 11m² (118ft²)** **Base coat ▶ 500ml yellow ochre milk (casein) paint (one coat)** **Wax coat ▶ 500ml beeswax or furniture wax (clear)** **Topcoat ▶ 500ml deep red milk (casein) paint**
EQUIPMENT	**2–3 x 50mm (2in) paint brushes / 1 x 25mm (1in) paint brush / wirewool / disposable gloves**
INSTRUCTIONS **Base coat**	ALWAYS WORK IN A WELL-VENTILATED AREA Stir the yellow ochre milk (casein) paint thoroughly. Using one of the 50mm (2in) paint brushes, apply an even coat to your prepared surface (see pp. 24–7) and allow to dry

❶ DEEP COLONIAL RED ON OCHRE
The basic recipe: deep tones and density of colour are common on Shaker woodwork. The pale base gives a wonderfully aged effect.

❷ ANTIQUE YELLOW ON SOLDIER BLUE
Another popular colourway: the main area of wear is the door knob, but the ageing can be more pronounced if you wish.

❸ OCHRE ON DEEP RED
This reverses the colours of the basic recipe for a less imposing effect.

❹ SOLDIER BLUE ON OCHRE
A lovely colour-mix and typical of the Shakers' pure hues, this would be good in a kitchen or in a bathroom.

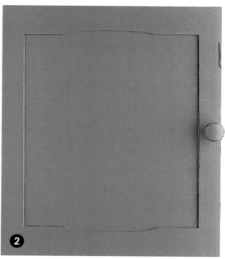

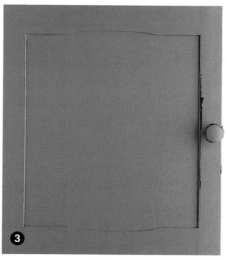

(24 hours). Milk paints create such a flat, smooth finish that you often do not need to add a second coat.

Wax coat

Brush a liberal coat of the beeswax onto the areas you wish to distress, using the 25mm (1in) paint brush. (The top-coat will not adhere permanently wherever there is a wax coating.) Allow to dry (1 hour).

Topcoat

1 Stir the deep red milk paint thoroughly and apply a good, even coat with a second 50mm (2in) paint brush. Allow to dry (24 hours).
2 Put on the gloves and rub the wirewool gently over the surface, concentrating on the areas where you applied the wax, until you reveal the ochre paint beneath.

These trugs were all painted with water-based materials. This gives more scope for colour variation, but do check picture references to maintain the correct feel. Almost all the colours described here are artists' acrylics and were added to 500ml vinyl silk emulsion.

The stone base coat for the brown and dusky pink trugs was coloured with 2tbsp yellow ochre. The brown topcoat tint was 3tbsp raw umber, 1tbsp yellow ochre and 1tbsp burnt umber. The dusky pink was made by mixing 2tbsp cadmium red, 1tbsp raw umber and 1/4tbsp cobalt blue.

The green was created with 3tbsp sap green and 1tbsp raw umber, and applied to the dusky pink described above. The blue was a premixed vinyl silk emulsion and was applied to a base coat coloured with 2tbsp cobalt blue.

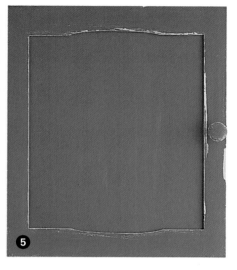

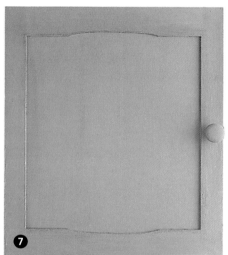

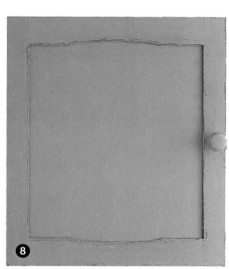

⑤ SEA GREEN ON WHITE
The green is made by adding 3tbsp chromium green and 1tbsp cobalt blue to 500ml white vinyl silk emulsion: a clean colourway with a different feel but still in the Shaker tradition.

⑥ TERRACOTTA ON GREY
This rich combination would make a good choice for a kitchen or bathroom. The terracotta is a premixed vinyl silk emulsion, but the base coat adds 2tbsp neutral grey to 500ml white vinyl silk emulsion.

⑦ CREAM ON PALE BLUE
A light colour-mix but again typical of Shaker taste: the base coat is made by adding 2tbsp cobalt blue to 500ml white vinyl silk emulsion; the cream by adding 2tbsp yellow ochre to 500ml white vinyl silk emulsion.

⑧ PALE BLUE ON TERRACOTTA
Another lively alternative: the base coat is the premixed terracotta used in sample 6, and the topcoat adds 3tbsp cobalt blue to 500ml white vinyl silk emulsion.

WATER-BASED SHAKER

Milk paints take a long time to dry so you may prefer to use water-based vinyl silk emulsion paints instead. These are now available in the deep colours of the Shaker palette, and may be more appealing in a small, dark room which could appear claustrophobic with surfaces given the dense, flat look of milk paint. Because of their less toxic qualities, emulsion paints are also the better option for a child's room.

Follow the quantities given in the basic recipe, using premixed paints or colouring 500ml vinyl silk emulsion with artists' acrylic colours. You may need two topcoats for a finish to equal that of milk paint. Allow 2–4 hours for each coat to dry. Use the beeswax and wirewool as indicated. For a hardwearing finish, seal with acrylic varnish, using a 50mm (2in) varnish brush, according to the manufacturers' instructions, but it is vital to remove all the wax first.

A convincing range of acrylic 'milk' paints is also available.

STONE FINISHES

Stone comes in many colours and textures, and reproducing it in paint can be complicated. Nevertheless, a reasonable resemblance to some of the less exotic stones is possible. The main pieces of equipment you need are nothing more than a household sponge and a bowl of water.

LIMESTONE

INGREDIENTS

To cover approximately 4m² (43ft²)
See swatch captions.

EQUIPMENT

3 or 4 containers / 2 or 3 x 75mm (3in) decorators' brushes / masking tape (optional) / coarse-textured paint roller plus tray / 2 or 3 household sponges / scissors / bowl of water / plant mister / methylated spirits / plate / short-haired fitch / stick

INSTRUCTIONS

❶ PINK LIMESTONE
The joint colour is 6tbsp white emulsion and 2tsp raw umber. For each of the following, begin with 6tbsp white emulsion. For the base colour, add ½tsp each yellow ochre and raw umber, for the first colour, 1tsp raw umber and 2tsp yellow ochre, and for the second colour, 2tsp neutral grey and ½tsp yellow ochre. Add dabs of yellow ochre, grey and white.

1 Prepare the surface thoroughly (see pp. 24–7). If you do not want joint lines, you should go straight to step 3. Otherwise, mix up the joint colour and brush it on in an uneven layer. Allow to dry (4 hours).

2 Using torn masking tape, mask out a pattern of ragged-edged joint lines over the painted surface.

3 Mix up the base colour and use the roller to apply one coat. Allow to dry (1 hour).

4 Trim two or three household sponges (see pp. 20–1).

5 Using the first colour, follow steps 3–5 on p.132.

6 If you want a finer texture, reduce the amount of water and use a plant mister to apply some of it. You can also work with a finer sponge.

7 A further variation is to splash or spray on methylated spirits. The water and colour will flow away from the methylated spirits, forming different shapes.

8 For colour variation, sponge on dabs of other suitable colours, but resist the temptation to overdo it. Once you have achieved the desired effect, allow to dry (1–2 hours), then remove any masking tape.

❷ GREY LIMESTONE
For the joints mix 4tbsp white and 2tbs black emulsion. The base coat is 6tbsp white emulsion and 2tsp neutral grey. The first colour is 4tbsp payne's grey, 2tbsp white and 4tsp burnt umber, while the second colour is white. For a more granular effect, we spattered on ¼tsp each of black and white, softened with a spray of methy-lated spirits.

9 Mix the second colour in a container and apply it in the same way as before, adding dabs of colour if you wish. Leave to dry thoroughly.

10 To create stone with a more granular appearance, spatter on black and white paint. Load a short-haired fitch with diluted paint and tap it hard against a stick held 30–40cm (12–16in) from your work. A long-haired brush will spatter everything around. The consistency of the paint is important. Too thin, and you will splash, not splatter; too thick, and the paint will not leave your brush.

SLATE

INGREDIENTS

To cover approximately 4m² (43ft²)
See swatch captions.

EQUIPMENT

1 or 2 containers / household sponge / masking tape / 1 x 75mm (3in) decorators' brush / spatula / wax

INSTRUCTIONS

1 Follow steps 1 and 2 above, but sponge on the joint colour instead of brushing it on.

2 Use the decorators' brush to apply one coat of the base colour and allow to dry (4 hours).

3 Mix the slate colour and use the spatula to apply it in a not-too-thick layer to a small area. Smooth out the paint using small circular movements. As it begins to dry, add a little wax and rub it in along with the paint. This burnishing action will give a hard, polished, slate-like finish. You will soon see when to add the wax, and discover how to make slight changes to the patina by varying your timing.

4 While still working on the first area, you can start to spread and burnish fresh paint alongside. You can work on two or three areas at the same time. Work across the whole surface without stopping, to avoid any joins showing. Allow to dry for a day.

❸ SLATE
The joint colour is the same mid-grey as grey limestone, while the slate base colour is 100ml black emulsion. The slate colour consists of 5tbsp payne's grey, 1tbsp white, 1tbsp phthalo-cyanine green and 2tsp burnt umber.

MARBLING

Marbling is perhaps the most well used of the stone finishes. It is possible, with careful study and practice, to reproduce accurate copies of any specific type, but in these recipes we show you how to create two *faux* or fantasy marbles. The method is less complicated and there is more room for artistic licence. However, even here a successful result depends on not overdoing the technique. And for 'authenticity' use picture references of real marble as a guide. Before you begin, decide on a basic pattern for the veining and other markings – it may be governed by the surface on which you are working – and keep the colours of your glazes close. Too much contrast makes for unconvincing results.

BASIC RECIPE – GREY FANTASY MARBLE

INGREDIENTS

To cover approximately 6m² (65ft²)
Base coat ▶ 500ml white oil-based eggshell paint / 2tbsp neutral grey artists' oil colour
First glaze coat ▶ 375ml oil-based scumble glaze (transparent) / 3tbsp zinc white artists' oil colour / 200ml white spirit (approx.)
Second glaze coat ▶ 375ml oil-based scumble glaze / 2tbsp neutral grey artists' oil colour / 1tbsp zinc white artists' oil colour / 200ml white spirit (approx.)
First veining ▶ 1tbsp black artists' oil colour / ¹/₂tbsp white spirit
Second veining ▶ 1tbsp yellow ochre artists' oil colour / ¹/₂tbsp white spirit
Sealant ▶ 500ml clear satin polyurethane varnish / 50g (1³/₄oz) french chalk

EQUIPMENT

3 large and 2 small containers for mixing paint and glaze / 2 x 50mm (2in) paint brushes / 2 x 25mm (1in) paint brushes / badger softener or dusting brush / fitch / swordliner or fine artists' brush / cloth

INSTRUCTIONS

ALWAYS WORK IN A WELL-VENTILATED AREA

Base coat

1 Pour the oil-based eggshell paint into one of the large containers. Add the neutral grey and stir well.
2 Apply an even coat to the prepared surface (see pp. 24–7) with a 50mm (2in) paint brush and allow to dry (24 hours).

First glaze coat

1 Pour the oil-based scumble into a second large container. Add the zinc white and 150ml white spirit (a little at a time), stirring well.
2 Apply to the base coat in diagonal, random strokes with one of the 25mm (1in) paint brushes, allowing about a quarter of the base coat to show through.
3 Skim lightly over the glaze with the badger softener (or dusting brush) to soften the brush strokes.
4 Using the fitch, flick some of the remaining white spirit onto the surface. Your aim is to disperse or spread the glaze a little, giving more depth to the effect.

Second glaze coat

1 Pour the oil-based scumble into a third large container. Add the neutral grey, zinc white, and 150ml white spirit (a little at a time), and stir well.

2 With the other 25mm (1in) paint brush, apply the second glaze randomly to some of the areas not covered by the first glaze coat. When you have finished, you should still be able to see parts of the base coat.

3 Repeat the softening process and again flick some of the remaining white spirit onto the glaze.

First veining

1 Place the black oil colour in one of the small containers. Add the white spirit (a little at a time) and stir well.

2 Using the swordliner (or fine artists' brush) to apply the solution, make a series of small, twisting lines on the wet glaze. Work diagonally across the surface but try to vary the path of each vein. Make some of them travel vertically, add 'branches' here and there, and continue them from one side of the surface to the other. It is important to avoid too uniform an effect if you want to achieve an authentic look.

❶ GREY MARBLE
The final stage of the basic recipe is about to begin: the veining stages are complete and the effect has been softened with a badger brush.

Sample A shows the first glaze stage: white glaze has been applied to some areas but parts of the base coat still show through. The glaze has been softened and then dispersed.

Sample B shows the second, darker glaze and first veining. Now black and white blend to produce authentic two-tone veins.

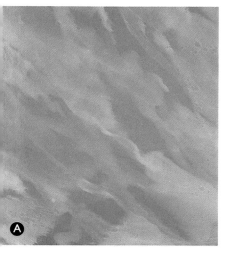

A

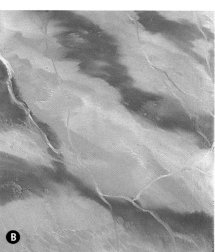

B

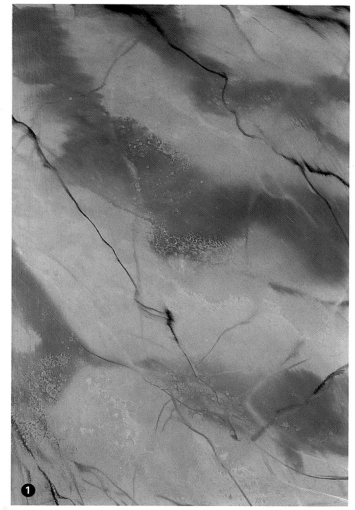

❶

MARBLING

The panelling in this room has been marbled using natural, sandy tones. This is a handsome demonstration of how successful and authentic a marble finish can be.

Second veining

1 Place the yellow ochre in the other small container. Add the white spirit (a little at a time) and stir well.

2 Create more veins – these should be smaller and fewer than the black veins of the previous stage.

3 Skim lightly over the yellow ochre veins with the softener. Allow to dry (24 hours).

Sealant coat

1 Apply one coat of varnish with the other 50mm (2in) paint brush, according to the manufacturers' instructions.

2 Sprinkle the french chalk onto the partially dry surface and buff up with a cloth – this helps to give the 'cloudy' appearance typical of real marble.

VARIATION – BLACK AND GOLD FANTASY MARBLE

INGREDIENTS

To cover approximately 8m² (86ft²)

Base coat ▶ 500ml black oil-based eggshell paint

First glaze coat ▶ 250ml oil-based scumble glaze (transparent) / 3tbsp zinc white artists' oil colour / 1tbsp oxide of chromium artists' oil colour / 200ml white spirit

Second glaze coat ▶ 250ml oil-based scumble glaze / 2tbsp zinc white artists' oil colour / 1tbsp yellow ochre artists' oil colour / 200ml white spirit

First veining ▶ 1tbsp oil-based scumble glaze / 1tbsp zinc white artists' oil colour / 1tbsp white spirit

Second veining ▶ 1tbsp oil-based scumble glaze / ¹⁄₂tbsp zinc white artists' oil colour / ¹⁄₂tbsp yellow ochre artists' oil colour / 1tbsp white spirit

Protective coat ▶ 500ml clear satin polyurethane or dead flat varnish

EQUIPMENT

2 x 50mm (2in) paint brushes / 2 large and 2 small containers for mixing glaze / 2 x 25mm (1in) paint brushes / badger softener or dusting brush / fitch / swordliner or fine artists' brush / cloth

INSTRUCTIONS

Base coat

ALWAYS WORK IN A WELL-VENTILATED AREA

Stir the oil-based eggshell paint well and apply an even coat to your prepared surface (see pp. 24–7) with one of the 50mm (2in) paint brushes. Allow to dry (24 hours).

First and second glaze coats

Follow the method in the Basic recipe, adding 150ml white spirit to the scumble and reserving 50ml to soften the glazes.

First and second veining

Follow the method in Basic recipe, First and Second veining, adding the oil colour and white spirit to the scumble.

Protective coat

Apply one coat of varnish with the other 50mm (2in) paint brush, according to the manufacturers' instructions.

2 BLACK AND GOLD MARBLE Bolder, more fantastic effects are a possibility with this type of finish, and the opportunity for experiment and colour variation is enormous. The glazes used here are thinner than those of the basic recipe and the result is a more translucent finish.

GRANITE

Granite was a stone traditionally used on the grand scale – for exterior decoration – but the paint finish can be used successfully on small features inside a modern or period home. This recipe uses sponging and spatter techniques to re-create granite's characteristic granular look. However, like many stones, it comes in different forms so study the real thing for an authentic effect. Table tops, pillars and garden ornaments and furniture are all potential projects.

BASIC RECIPE – GRANITE

INGREDIENTS

To cover approximately 6m² (65ft²)

Base coat ► 500ml white vinyl matt emulsion / 2tbsp neutral grey artists' acrylic colour

First glaze coat ► 100ml white vinyl matt emulsion / 2tbsp neutral grey artists' acrylic colour / 1tbsp burnt umber artists' acrylic colour / 2tbsp water / methylated spirits (see instructions)

Second glaze coat ► 100ml white vinyl matt emulsion / 2tbsp water / methylated spirits

First spatter coat ► 1tbsp mars black artists' acrylic colour / 1tbsp water

Second spatter coat ► 1tbsp zinc white artists' acrylic colour / 1tbsp water methylated spirits

Protective coat ► 500ml clear satin acrylic varnish

EQUIPMENT

3 large and 2 small containers for mixing paint and glaze / 1 x 50mm (2in) decorators' brush / 3 sea sponges / water to dampen sponges / flower mister / 2 fitches / 1 x 50mm (2in) varnish brush

INSTRUCTIONS
Base coat

1 Pour the emulsion into one of the large containers. Add the neutral grey and stir well.
2 Apply evenly to the prepared surface (see pp. 24–7), using the 50mm (2in) decorators' brush. Allow to dry (2–4 hours).

First glaze coat

1 Pour the emulsion into another large container. Add the neutral grey, burnt umber and water (little by little). Stir well.
2 Immerse one of the sponges in water and wring out. Using the damp sponge, apply glaze to the entire surface in light, dabbing movements.
3 Half fill the flower mister with methylated spirits and spray a fine mist over the surface. This causes the glaze to disperse or spread slightly, producing a more interesting texture. Allow to dry (2 hours).

Above left: This tub, made of heavy-duty plastic, was bought cheaply at a garden centre and painted as described in the recipe. Its basic shape recalls that of a traditional garden urn so it makes an ideal subject for a stone effect, and the finish helps to disguise the fussy detail on the lip.

Second glaze coat

1 Pour the emulsion into a third large container. Add the water (a little at a time), stirring well.

2 Apply to the entire surface with a second damp sponge in the same way.

3 Again using the flower mister, spray methylated spirits onto the glazed surface.

4 While the glaze is still wet, sponge again, using a third damp sponge, and carefully blend the two colours.

First spatter coat

1 Place the mars black in one of the small containers. Add the water (a little at a time) and stir well.

2 Load one of the fitches with glaze. Holding a clean fitch in one hand and the loaded fitch in the other, tap the handle of the loaded brush against the handle of the other so that flecks of paint spatter onto the surface. You are aiming for a fine haze of dots, applied more densely in some areas than in others.

Second spatter coat

1 Place the zinc white in the other small container. Add the water (a little at a time) and stir well.

2 Again spatter the surface with fine dots, using the second fitch and aiming for a random, uneven effect.

3 Using the flower mister, spray a fine mist of methylated spirits over the surface. Allow to dry (2 hours).

Protective coat

Apply one coat of varnish, using the varnish brush, according to the manufacturers' instructions.

Exterior use Substitute two coats of satin polyurethane varnish for protection, according to the manufacturers' instructions.

❶ GRANITE
The effect of the basic recipe on a flat surface: this finish would work well on panelling or on a table top. You could also try it on a plain, formal mantelpiece or fire surround.

TERRACOTTA

Terracotta's chalky look is widely used for garden containers. However, some of the largest pots are expensive and, because they have a limited lifespan, the possibility of creating durable reproductions is attractive. Authenticity is achieved with simple dripping and sponging techniques: work the surface hard to enhance the effect. Objects with detail are especially successful because you can add extra ageing in the crevices. This finish is perfect for containers but works well on surfaces too.

BASIC RECIPE – TERRACOTTA

INGREDIENTS

To cover approximately 6m² (65ft²)
First base coat ▶ 500ml white vinyl matt emulsion / 2tbsp yellow ochre artists' acrylic colour / 1tbsp raw sienna artists' acrylic colour
Second base coat ▶ 500ml white vinyl matt emulsion / 2tbsp venetian red artists' acrylic colour / 2tbsp raw umber artists' acrylic colour / 1tbsp bronze ochre artists' acrylic colour
Glaze coat ▶ 100ml white vinyl matt emulsion / 150ml water

EQUIPMENT

3 containers for mixing paint and glaze / 2 x 50mm (2in) decorators' brushes / stippling or block brush / water to dampen brush and sponge / 1 x 25mm (1in) round fitch / sea sponge

INSTRUCTIONS
First base coat

1 Pour the emulsion into one of the containers. Add the yellow ochre and raw sienna and stir well.
2 Apply evenly to your prepared surface (see pp. 24–7) with a 50mm (2in) decorators' brush. Leave to dry (2–4 hours).

Second base coat

1 Pour the emulsion into a second container. Add the venetian red, raw umber and bronze ochre and stir well.
2 Apply to the surface, using the other 50mm (2in) decorators' brush, with random strokes, allowing some of the base coat to show through. Leave to dry (2–4 hours).

❶ TERRACOTTA
Here the terracotta finish is applied to a flat surface and a three-dimensional detail (a plaster shape from a ceiling rose). Note how ageing on the irregular areas adds to the weathered effect. Plaster and plastic are ideal surfaces for the terracotta finish.

Three plastic pots were prepared and painted using the technique described in the basic terracotta recipe. They were finished with two coats of satin polyurethane varnish and sunk into the wet plaster of a roughly textured wall colourwashed (see p. 48) in a soft pink. Masonry nails driven through the back of the pots into the wall will give extra security.

Glaze coat

1 Pour the emulsion into a third container. Add the water (a little at a time), stirring well.

2 Dip the stippling (or block) brush in water and, with a light, tapping action, dampen the painted surface.

3 Hold or place the object in an upright position. Using the fitch, drip the glaze vertically down the surface – you are imitating the action of weathering. Repeat to cover the surface.

4 Immerse the sponge in water and wring out. Dab it lightly over the glaze to take up the excess water as the surface begins to dry to a chalky finish. Allow to dry (2 hours).

Exterior use Finish with two coats of satin polyurethane varnish, according to the manufacturers' instructions.

PATINATION ON METAL

When exposed to the elements metal fittings and architectural details tarnish and corrode over time. The results are often beautiful, evoking a wonderful sense of history, and craftsmen have now developed ways of reproducing patination on new metal. Some methods are complex and use dangerous chemicals, but cold-patination fluids (available for a variety of metals) are less dangerous, easier to use and create natural effects. Try experimenting with inexpensive candlesticks: the results can be effective. The key to success is timing – the process works very quickly – but it is a lot easier than waiting years for an object to age naturally or burying it in the garden. While these fluids are not as dangerous as most chemical methods, they are still toxic, so take care.

BASIC RECIPE – COLD PATINATION ON BRASS

INGREDIENTS

For three candlesticks
300ml methylated spirits / 200ml brown cold-patination fluid for brass, copper and bronze
Optional protective coat ▶ 200ml clear wax or oil fixative

EQUIPMENT

Cottonwool balls / water for rinsing / rubber gloves / protective mask / wirewool / rags (optional)

INSTRUCTIONS

WEAR GLOVES AND MASK WHEN USING COLD-PATINATION FLUIDS. FOLLOW MANUFACTURERS' INSTRUCTIONS AND WORK IN A WELL-VENTILATED AREA.

1 Clean the surface with cottonwool balls soaked in methylated spirits. Rinse in water and allow to dry (2 hours).
2 Put on the rubber gloves and protective mask. Rub clean cottonwool balls soaked in cold-patination fluid over the surface. It works very quickly – the metal changes colour as the fluid goes on. Rinse the surface in fresh water as soon as you have the colour you want. Leave it too long and it will be very dark. Never leave the fluid on for more than 2 minutes.

❸ ON COPPER
Another patination fluid gives an authentic verdigris effect in seconds. Again follow the basic recipe, applying the fluid with cottonwool or stippling it on with a soft brush. A second coat gives a more 'crusty' feel.

❶ ON BRASS
The basic method: only the middle of this sample is worked with wirewool, leaving the softer, aged effect at the edges.

❷ ON STEEL
This shows the use of the black cold-patination fluid for steel and iron. Simply follow the quantities and method given in the basic recipe.

3 As soon as you have rinsed the surface, rub it gently with the wirewool to remove the colour until you have the effect you want. Rinse in fresh water and allow to dry (1 hour).

Notes For a more hardwearing finish, rub wax (or oil fixative) over the entire surface with rags and allow to dry (1 hour).
Exterior use Apply one coat of oil fixative to the surface in the method described above.

Instant ageing and antiquing: these inexpensive candlesticks and holders have been patinated with the fluids used in the basic recipe and samples.

RUST

Probably the most extreme of the metal finishes, this look of age and corrosion is very popular. Our recipe, which uses water-based materials, is fast, safe and simple, and you can, of course, vary the technique to enhance the impression of age. For example, you can simply apply both coats more heavily, remembering that for authenticity the effect must be uneven. Or give the rust more texture by adding about 70g (2½oz) fine sand to the base coat. It works well on metal, but can be applied to various surfaces.

BASIC RECIPE – RUST

INGREDIENTS

To cover approximately 6m² (65ft²)
Base coat ▶ 500ml premixed black vinyl matt emulsion / 2tbsp titanium white artists' acrylic colour / 2tbsp ultramarine blue artists' acrylic colour
First rust coat ▶ 100ml raw sienna artists' acrylic colour / 3tbsp venetian red artists' acrylic colour / 1tbsp burnt umber artists' acrylic colour / 1tbsp red oxide artists' acrylic colour
Second rust coat ▶ 100ml yellow ochre artists' acrylic colour / 2tbsp yellow oxide artists' acrylic colour / 1tbsp raw sienna artists' acrylic colour

EQUIPMENT

3 containers for mixing paint / 1 x 50mm (2in) decorators' brush / 2 x 25mm (1in) round fitches

INSTRUCTIONS
Base coat

1 Pour the emulsion into one of the containers. Add the titanium white and ultramarine and stir well.
2 Apply an even coat (see pp. 24–7) to your prepared surface with the decorators' brush and allow to dry (2–4 hours).

First rust coat

1 Place the raw sienna, venetian red, burnt umber and red oxide in a second container and stir well.
2 Using a fitch, stipple the mix onto the surface with a gentle tapping action. Allow a little of the basecoat to show through. Leave to dry (1 hour).

Second rust coat

1 Put yellow ochre, yellow oxide and raw sienna in a third container and stir.
2 Using the other fitch, again stipple the mix onto the surface. Apply this coat more heavily, although parts of the other coats must remain visible. Build up the colour in some areas to avoid a uniform finish. Allow to dry (1 hour).

Exterior use Finish with two coats of matt polyurethane varnish, according to the manufacturers' instructions.

❶ RUST
This inexpensive metal table was an ideal subject. Detail (as in the coat-of-arms, above left) always lends itself to the technique. Ageing has been increased with two applications to the top and rim.

VERDIGRIS

Verdigris is perhaps the most stunning of the weathering effects to be seen on metal, occurring naturally on copper and bronze in the characteristic streaks of salty, acidic greens and whites. Simulating this effect originally involved the use of extremely toxic chemicals and intense heat (see also the less hazardous cold-patination technique for verdigris explained on p. 104). However, this recipe uses water-based products so it is much safer and easier. You can increase the aged effect by working the surface over and over again.

The finish can be applied to many surfaces so hunt out all sorts of unusual objects to work on. Anything with lots of detail will pick up the look wonderfully well, although the method works on a flat surface just as successfully. Look at the real thing on statues and metalwork which have been exposed to the elements for years.

This decorative weather-vane is a good example of the verdigris effect. It has added to the character of the piece and, as the vane would once have been used outdoors, verdigris is an obvious and appropriate choice.

BASIC RECIPE – VERDIGRIS

INGREDIENTS

To cover approximately 6m² (65ft²)
Base coat ► 500ml blackboard paint or premixed black vinyl matt emulsion
First verdigris coat ► 2tbsp titanium white artists' acrylic colour / 2tbsp viridian green artists' acrylic colour / 4tbsp water / methylated spirits
Second verdigris coat ► 2tbsp titanium white acrylic artists' colour / 1tbsp yellow ochre artists' acrylic colour / 100ml water / methylated spirits
Sealant/finishing coat ► 500ml clear matt acrylic varnish / 25g (9/10oz) whiting or chalk powder

EQUIPMENT

1 x 50mm (2in) decorators' brush / 2 containers for mixing paint / 3 x 25mm (1in) round fitches / flower mister / 1 x 50mm (2in) varnish brush / rags

VERDIGRIS

INSTRUCTIONS

Base coat

Stir the blackboard or emulsion paint well and apply an even coat to the prepared surface (see pp. 24–7) using the decorators' brush. Allow to dry (2–4 hours).

First verdigris coat

1 Place the titanium white and viridian green in one of the containers. Add the water (a little at a time) and stir well.
2 Load one of the fitches with the solution and, holding or positioning the object vertically, dribble the liquid onto the surface so it drips downwards. Repeat to cover the surface.
3 Half fill the flower mister with methylated spirits and spray a fine mist onto the surface to disperse the paint slightly.

Second verdigris coat

1 Place the titanium white and yellow ochre in the other container. Add 50ml water (a little at a time) and stir well.
2 Using a second fitch, dribble the solution in the same way.
3 Spray a fine mist of methylated spirits, as described above.
4 Dribble the remaining water onto the vertical surface as before, using a third fitch, until you have the effect you want. Allow to dry (2 hours).

Sealant/finishing coat

1 Brush one coat of varnish onto the entire surface, using the 50mm (2in) varnish brush, and leave to become tacky (approx. 20 minutes).
2 Rub in some whiting (or chalk powder), paying particular attention to any detail. This helps to give an authentic 'chalky' finish. Wipe off any loose, excess whiting with rags according to the manufacturers' instructions.

Exterior use Add two coats of satin polyurethane varnish, allowing 24 hours for each coat to dry.

Opposite: This impressive lion-head fountain is, in fact, made of plastic, transformed by the use of the verdigris effect. It was prepared and primed with two coats of blackboard paint. To protect a surface from regular exposure to water, add two or three coats of yacht varnish after the sealant/ finishing coat, according to the manufacturers' instructions.

❶ VERDIGRIS
The basic recipe applied to a flat surface and three-dimensional detail: you can, if you prefer, substitute 500ml premixed rust emulsion for blackboard paint in the base coat. The effect is similar.

LEAD

Aged, weathered lead has a grey-blue, salty or chalky appearance, the result of chemical changes in the metal. It is a look that is easily created with water-based products – simply by dripping coloured glazes onto a vertical surface and then ageing with whiting. Plastic flower pots and troughs are ideal subjects, but plain, cheap metal items are equally effective and will look wonderfully expensive. As with most of the metal effects, you choose how much to age the finish.

BASIC RECIPE – LEAD

INGREDIENTS

To cover approximately 6m² (65ft²)
Sealant coat ▶ 500ml PVA adhesive or white glue / 500ml water
Base coat ▶ 500ml white vinyl matt emulsion / 1tbsp burnt umber artists' acrylic colour / 1tbsp premixed black vinyl matt emulsion
First glaze ▶ 4tbsp premixed black vinyl matt emulsion / 2tbsp titanium white artists' acrylic colour / ¹/₂tbsp burnt umber artists' acrylic colour / 150ml water
Second glaze coat ▶ 5tbsp titanium white artists' acrylic colour / 2tbsp burnt umber artists' acrylic colour / 1tbsp ultramarine blue artists' acrylic colour / 150ml water
Sealant/finishing coat ▶ 500ml PVA adhesive or white glue / 500ml water / 50g (1³/₄oz) whiting or chalk powder

EQUIPMENT

5 containers for mixing paint and glaze / 2 x 25mm (1in) decorators' brushes / 3 x 50mm (2in) decorators' brushes / 1 x 25mm (1in) round fitch / rags

INSTRUCTIONS
Sealant coat

1 Pour the PVA adhesive (or white glue) into one of the containers. Add the water (a little at a time) and stir well.
2 Brush the solution onto your prepared surface, using one of the 25mm (1in) decorators' brushes. Allow to dry (1 hour).

Base coat

1 Pour the white emulsion into a second container. Add the burnt umber and black emulsion and stir well.
2 Apply evenly to the prepared surface (see pp. 24–7) with 50mm (2in) decorators' brush and allow to dry (2–4 hours).

❶ LEAD
The classic effect: highly successful on flat surfaces and relief detailing so you can, for example, convert cheap plastic into something a great deal more splendid. Success depends partly on finding an appropriate design.

The inexpensive metal sconce on the left of the picture has been changed beyond recognition by the application of the lead effect described in the basic recipe.

First glaze coat

1 Pour the emulsion into a third container. Add the white, burnt umber, and 100ml water (a little at a time). Stir well.
2 Apply the glaze to the entire surface with random strokes, using a second 50mm (2in) decorators' brush.
3 Load the fitch with water and, holding the object vertically, drip the liquid onto the surface so it runs from top to bottom. This helps to disperse the glaze, allowing some of the base to show through. Repeat to cover. Allow to dry (1 hour).

Second glaze coat

1 Put the titanium white, burnt umber and ultramarine in a fourth container. Add 100ml water (a little at a time) and stir.
2 Using a third 50mm (2in) brush, apply with random cross-hatched strokes. Parts of the other coats must remain visible.
3 Drip water onto the surface again. Allow to dry (2 hours).

Sealant/finishing coat

1 Put the PVA adhesive (or white glue) in a fifth container. Add the water (a little at a time) and stir well.
2 Apply to the entire surface with the other 25mm (1in) decorators' brush and leave until it is tacky (5–7 minutes).
3 Rub the whiting (or chalk powder) into the surface, using rags. Pay special attention to any detail. Remove excess whiting with clean rags. Allow to dry (2–3 hours).

Exterior use Add two coats of matt polyurethane varnish, according to the manufacturers' instructions.

TORTOISESHELL

This effect simulates the appearance of the shell of the sea turtle, which was first used as a decorative veneer in the East. Imitated for centuries, the pattern is created with diagonal strokes on different background colours, such as white, cinnamon and gold. The latter was once real gold leaf but Dutch metal leaf or gold sprays are just as successful. This recipe reproduces the classic colours. It works well on small, flat surfaces – the shell cannot be carved – but it is striking on screens and table tops.

BASIC RECIPE – UMBER AND OCHRE

INGREDIENTS

To cover approximately 6m² (65ft²)
Base coat ▶ 500ml white vinyl matt emulsion / 3tbsp raw sienna artists' acrylic colour
Glaze coats ▶ 3tbsp yellow ochre artists' acrylic colour / 3tbsp raw sienna artists' acrylic colour / 3tbsp burnt umber artists' acrylic colour / 500ml acrylic scumble glaze (transparent) / 150ml water
Spatter coat ▶ 1tbsp burnt umber artists' acrylic colour / 3¹/₃tbsp water
Protective coat ▶ 500ml clear satin acrylic varnish

EQUIPMENT

Container for mixing paint / 1 x 50mm (2in) decorators' brush / 4 saucers for mixing glaze / 1 x 50mm (2in) paint brush / 3 x 25mm (1in) flat artists' brushes / badger softener or dusting brush / disposable gloves / toothbrush / 1 x 50mm (2in) varnish brush

INSTRUCTIONS
Base coat

1 Pour the emulsion into the container. Add the raw sienna and stir well.
2 Apply an even coat to your prepared surface (see pp. 24–7) with the decorators' brush and allow to dry (2–4 hours).

An interesting example of the use of the tortoiseshell finish, the little lampshade blends delightfully with the surrounding objets d'art and antiques. The effect could easily be reproduced on a simple metal shade.

❶ UMBER AND OCHRE
The basic-recipe colourway: the sample is painted on an area larger than is normally undertaken, but it illustrates well the potential use of tortoiseshell on flat surfaces, such as small decorative panels or trays.

Glaze coats

1 Place each of the three colours on a separate saucer. Add 50ml acrylic scumble and 50ml water (a little at a time) to each colour and stir well. Set aside.

2 Apply the remaining 350ml acrylic scumble in a thin, even coat to the base coat, using the paint brush.

3 Using one of the artists' brushes, apply the yellow ochre glaze to the surface in random, diagonal strokes. You are aiming for a rough, 'daubed' effect with much of the base coat still showing through.

4 Repeat the process, using a different brush for each of the remaining, darker colours. Brush glaze onto other random areas until the base coat is completely covered.

5 Skim lightly over the surface with the badger softener (or dusting brush), allowing the hairs of the brush to touch the glaze. Your aim is to remove the brush strokes and to merge the colours into each other to create the tortoiseshell effect. Allow to dry (24 hours).

These simple boxes illustrate a variation of the basic recipe in colours often found in tortoise-shell. The base coat was a premixed deep red emulsion; in the glaze coats 3tbsp cadmium red replaced the yellow ochre; the spatter and protective coats were unchanged.

Spatter coat

1 Place the burnt umber on the fourth saucer. Add the water (a little at a time) and stir.

2 Put on the disposable gloves. Load the toothbrush with paint. Holding it about 20cm (8in) from the surface, flick back the bristles with the fingers of your other hand to produce a fine mist of paint. You are aiming for little patches of dots rather than the even coverage typical of spattering. Allow to dry (4–5 hours).

Protective coat

Using the varnish brush, apply one coat of varnish according to the manufacturers' instructions.

BRONZING

Bronzing is an ancient technique used as an alternative or supplementary method to gilding (see p. 116). An object or area is sized and a fine metallic powder, originally real gold, is brushed or blown onto it to produce a subtly bronzed, antique look. The powders are very fine and toxic so always wear a mask and take care. Try not to use too much at a time to avoid waste and mess. Many colours and tones are available: most tones of gold, bronze and copper are easily found and other colours, such as purple, green and red, can be bought in specialist shops.

Bronzing can be used on a variety of surfaces and many objects. The technique produces an opulent look that is great for transforming old or second-hand objects. Metal chairs and other garden ornaments are ideal. So, too, are plaster architectural mouldings and statues. It is also an excellent way of applying subtle decoration to painted items. Just mask the areas you want to protect and follow the recipe. The powders tend to spread so do not use them on newly painted or varnished areas.

BASIC RECIPE – DEEP GOLD

INGREDIENTS

To cover approximately 3m² (32ft²)
Base coat ▶ 250ml red oxide primer
Bronzing ▶ 250ml water-based size / 75g (2²/₃oz) deep gold bronze powder
Protective coat ▶ 250ml amber french enamel varnish

EQUIPMENT

2 x 25mm (1in) paint brushes / protective mask / 1 x 25mm (1in) flat artists' brush / small, soft-bristled brush / soft cloths / 1 x 25mm (1in) varnish brush

❶ DEEP GOLD
The basic recipe: a rich, yet subtle effect.

❷ COPPER
This variation follows the basic recipe, simply substituting copper bronze powder at the bronzing stage and red french enamel varnish for the protective coat.

INSTRUCTIONS

Base coat

ALWAYS WEAR A MASK AND WORK IN A WELL-VENTILATED AREA
Stir the red oxide primer well and apply an even coat to your prepared surface (see pp. 24–7), using one of the paint brushes. Allow to dry (24 hours).

Bronzing

1 Shake or stir the size according to the manufacturers' instructions. Apply a thin, even coat to the base coat, using

Bronzing a metal chair, following a variation of the basic recipe.

A rust inhibitor and metal primer were applied first, and then came two coats of premixed black oil-based primer (250ml each). Light gold bronze powder was stirred into the size at the bronzing stage, and the protective coat was a neutral french enamel varnish.

A final coat of satin polyurethane varnish was added, according to the manufacturers' instructions, for extra protection as the chair was to be used outside.

the other paint brush. Allow to become tacky and transparent (approx. 20–30 minutes).

2 Put on the protective mask. Using the artists' brush, take up a little of the bronze powder at a time and brush it carefully onto the surface until most of the base coat is covered.

3 Gently remove some of the excess powder with the soft-bristled brush.

4 Rub carefully with soft cloths to burnish.

rotective coat   Apply one coat of varnish to the surface, using the varnish brush, and allow to dry (1 hour).

GILDING

Real gold leaf is both costly and time consuming to use, and today there are a variety of alternatives (see p. 19). Dutch metal leaf is the most convincing, being also cheaper and simpler to apply, and the modern gold sizes – Italian (water-based) and Japan (oil-based) – are effective and faster drying than the traditional substances. To give a smooth surface for gilding, a gesso is traditionally applied, tinted red to give a good base colour to the leaf. Gesso can be bought ready mixed or a modern version made of whiting and PVA adhesive. But it is simpler and equally effective to substitute, as this recipe does, a coat of red oxide primer or deep red emulsion. Gilding is ideal for plaster mouldings, picture and mirror frames, candlesticks and a variety of other ornaments.

❶ CLASSIC AGEING
This plaster leaf is gilded using the Dutch metal leaf method described in the basic recipe. Here the ageing glaze is grey.

❷ OLD GOLD
The ageing glaze for this leaf is coloured with 2tbsp yellow ochre mixed with 1tbsp acra gold. This tone brings out the richness of the metal leaf and is reminiscent of the Italian gold used on many religious paintings.

❸ PALE GOLD
The base coat is pre-mixed dark green vinyl matt emulsion. The ageing glaze is tinted with 1tbsp coeruleum blue and 1¹/₂tbsp titanium white. The green base gives the gold a thinner tone.

❹ MODERN GOLD
This ageing glaze is simply coloured with 2tbsp dioxazine purple and is a more contemporary way of treating a gilded object.

BASIC RECIPE – GOLD DUTCH METAL WITH CLASSIC AGEING

INGREDIENTS

For one plaster leaf moulding
Base coat ▶ 250ml red oxide primer or deep red vinyl matt emulsion
Sizing coat ▶ 250ml Italian water-based or quick-drying Japan gold size
Gilding ▶ 12 gold Dutch metal leaves
Optional additional ageing ▶ 2tbsp methylated spirit
Sealant coat ▶ 250ml amber shellac
Ageing glaze ▶ 2tbsp white vinyl silk emulsion / ¹/₂tbsp neutral grey artists' acrylic colour / ¹/₂tbsp yellow ochre artists' acrylic colour / 2tbsp water

EQUIPMENT

3 x 25mm (1in) decorators' brushes / bowl / disposable gloves / 1 x 25mm (1in) round, very soft-bristled brush / 2 soft polishing cloths / wirewool (optional) / 1 x 25mm (1in) varnish brush / container for mixing glaze / rags

INSTRUCTIONS
Base coat

Stir the primer (or emulsion) well and, using one of the decorators' brushes, apply an even coat to your prepared surface (see pp. 24–7). Allow to dry (2–4 hours).

Sizing coat

Shake or stir the size, following the manufacturers' instructions. Using a second decorators' brush, apply a thin but even coat of size to the entire surface. Never overload the brush because it is important to leave as few bubbles on the surface as possible. Allow the size to dry a little (20–30 minutes) until it becomes transparent and tacky.

Gilding

1 Place the bowl on your work surface with the metal leaves close at hand.
2 Put on the gloves and hold the object over the bowl to catch any broken leaf. Lift up each leaf and lay it carefully on the surface. Cover the object completely, or, for an aged effect, allow some of the primer to show through.
3 Use the soft-bristled brush to dust the object lightly, brushing the excess leaf into the bowl. You can use small pieces to cover gaps and keep larger ones for another project.
4 Rub the surface gently with one of the polishing cloths until it is smooth and shiny. Take care not to rub too hard or too much or the leaf will lift off.

Sealant coat

Using the varnish brush, apply a thin but even coat of shellac to the surface to deepen the colour. This is important as Dutch metal can look tinny. Leave to dry (45 minutes).

Ageing glaze

1 Pour the emulsion into the container and add the neutral grey and yellow ochre. Stir thoroughly and then add the water (a little at a time), mixing again.

2 Using a third decorators' brush, dab the entire surface with glaze and then quickly rub off with rags so that the glaze remains only in the detailing.

3 Rub the gilding on the raised and highlighted areas with the other soft polishing cloth to buff up. Allow the remaining emulsion to dry (30 minutes).

Notes You can increase the ageing effect by gently taking back the gilding in places where the object would naturally become worn. Use a little wirewool dipped in methylated spirits before applying the sealant coat.

Gilding transforms a galvanized garden tub: a blue metal primer designed for car paintwork substitutes for red oxide in the base coat. About 20 gold Dutch metal leaves were applied and sealed with amber shellac. The ageing glaze was coloured simply with 4tbsp coeruleum blue.

118

VARIATION – GOLD BROKEN LEAF

⑤ GOLD BROKEN LEAF
Follow the basic recipe for the base coat, sizing and gilding stages. You will need 100g (3¹/₂oz) broken leaf. Seal with a diluted amber french enamel varnish (170ml varnish to 80ml methylated spirits), using a 50mm (2in) paint brush. Allow to dry (30 minutes).

As the name suggests, broken leaf is composed of the off-cuts and fragments created when making Dutch metal leaf. Gold and aluminium (see below) are available. You buy it by weight and it is cheaper than whole leaf. Broken leaf takes much longer to apply – to be honest, it takes some patience – but done well it creates a more worn, aged effect because more of the base coat shows through. There is no need to apply an ageing glaze.

VARIATION – COPPER LEAF

⑥ COPPER LEAF
As basic recipe for base coat, sizing and gilding, using 12 copper leaves. Seal with 250ml clear satin acrylic varnish, applied with a 50mm (2in) brush. Allow to dry (1 hour). Finish with a blue ageing coat (2tbsp white vinyl silk emulsion, /2tbsp neutral grey, scant 1tsp ultramarine blue and 2tbsp water).

Theatricality is really the keynote here, although copper Dutch metal leaf gives a less opulent effect than the more traditional gold leaf. We think it works well in contemporary interiors, and in particular with more unusual *objets d'art* and ethnic collections. If you have a taste for the less predictable, you could experiment with coloured French enamel varnishes for the sealant coat (see sample 5 for the proportions). We have sometimes used bright red to create an exciting, modern effect.

VARIATION – ALUMINIUM LEAF

⑦ ALUMINIUM LEAF
The process and quantities are as for the basic recipe, but use a premixed blue vinyl matt emulsion for the base coat, seal with transparent acrylic crumble glaze instead of shellac, and omit the yellow ochre from the ageing ingredients.

Aluminium Dutch metal leaf is used to create a silver-leaf finish. Again, like copper leaf, it seems to suit modern interiors best. Premixed blue or green vinyl matt emulsion is substituted for red oxide primer (or deep red emulsion) at the base-coat stage because either will complement the silver well. In the sample shown here we used a mid-tone blue, but if you like bold effects try experimenting with the darker tones of either colour.

PART THREE

DECORATIVE DESIGNS & FINISHES

An introduction to the techniques you will need for applying both paint and pattern, together with ideas on how to incorporate them into simple and effective designs in a range of colours.

An example of what can be achieved using a combination of techniques. The fossil set in granite (see pp. 163–5) is made by combining stone effects, stencilling and a whiting resist. The result is an elegant and unusual table top.

INTRODUCTION

In Parts Three and Four we set out to show how colour, texture and pattern can come together in designs which have a certain vitality, whether it be radiated out in highly charged contrasts or in a quiet and stylish manner. Here in over 70 paint recipes are a variety of decorative techniques, designs and projects that can be followed, like a cookery recipe, teaspoon for teaspoon, or used as a point of departure for you to develop and realize your own ideas.

In Part Three we include the techniques you will need for the project and design ideas in Parts Three and Four. These are simply ways of applying and manipulating paint to create a range of surface textures, from flat matt to highly decorative. To these techniques we have added stamping, stencilling and the use of masking and resists – all methods of producing and/or reproducing a design in a controlled manner.

All the techniques are simple. None requires specialist knowledge or expensive equipment and they can usually be mastered quickly. In the case of the stencils and stamps, we have kept our designs simple too so they are easy to cut and apply. We have aimed to use all our techniques in a way that gives a great deal of freedom, providing a result that looks fresh and contemporary.

Gaining confidence in handling your materials and equipment is all part of the pleasure of decorating. There is no doubt that the best way to do this is to practise. Use an area of wall that can be painted over afterwards, or offcuts of plasterboard, which is what was used for many of the examples in this book. These have the extra advantage that you can pick them up and move them around, since colours will change their appearance in different lights and according to their position in a room.

Although we have chosen the equipment and materials to be as simple as possible, there will always remain, for those who want to abandon plain white interiors for decorative paint effects, the difficult question of which colours to choose. Decisions about colour are always going to give pause for reflection. There was a time when rules of taste gave guidance, but at the beginning of a new century almost all of these have been rejected. Blue with green can now be seen. You may choose colours because of the memories they evoke, for cultural reasons or because they are soothing. These choices are all personal and only you make them. You may seek guidance in colour theory, but understanding the spectrum and how to mix paint will not be much help in choosing which colours to use, although it can explain why certain colour combinations behave in the way they do. We know of only one artist who derives inspiration from the colour wheel. The rest spend more time looking at other painters' work.

We believe a lot can be learnt by looking, and this partly explains why we give such a broad range of colour combinations. We usually show two or three alternative colourways for each design. Even the basic techniques are shown in alternative colourways, as well as with some additional decorative device – whether it be to manipulate them into stripes or panels, or to add a masked-out motif. This not only gives you a choice, but we hope it will let you see the effect a change of colour, be it ever so small, can have. You also have the option to use a recipe from elsewhere in the book if it is more in keeping with your scheme. Whatever you do, always look at other interiors, at textiles, clothing and painting, and take your lead from those you like.

Interiors, like the colours we wear, are influenced by fashion, except that we often have to live in buildings which were built many decades ago. Do not let this trouble you. With care we can combine the old with the new. You can have respect for the old, even venerate it, but that does not mean you have to live in a time-warp. Nevertheless, we personally have been influenced by a lot of what we have seen from the past, not least because the colours of old, derived from natural pigments, have a quality we happen to like.

Apart from the task of choosing and mixing colours, you will have to arrange them into shapes on your surface. In the realm of pattern, fashion again exerts its influence, but the mood is a lot more individual than it was twenty years ago – softer yet full of vitality. The fleur-de-lis of old has been replaced by the altogether more lively spiral.

Some design classics will always remain, but they can be adapted to suit the current mood or look. One example of this is stripes. These seem to change their personality each season. One year all slim and Regency, they reappear the next as broad and Gustavian. Whatever form they take, you know that stripes will bring a great sense of style to a room. While stripes seem to go naturally on a wall, checks gravitate all too readily onto the floor. This is not a hard and fast rule, though, so try applying your checks to walls, window surrounds or even furniture.

Applying checks and stripes needs only the skills of planning and layout, and maybe some dexterous use of masking tape. Other designs can be helped onto wall or floor with stencils and stamps. These are an excellent way of controlling where your paint goes, as well as a means of covering a surface quickly. In most cases, at the back of this book we give the motifs for the stencils and stamps we use because we realize that many of you will lack the confidence to develop a pattern or draw a motif. You can very easily trace and enlarge our motifs to the size you require, then transfer them to your surface.

If you like what you see here, you can incorporate it straight away in your own decorating. Otherwise, you could take one technique – say dry brushing – and use it as the background to a stencilled or stamped design. Or, if you like a technique but not our choice of colours, experiment using a colour recipe from elsewhere in the book. We hope we have provided you with a starting point. The rest is up to you.

COLOURWASHED STRIPES

Colourwashing is probably one of the most useful techniques in decorative painting. We have made much use of it throughout Parts Three and Four, either as a background to the motifs, or for the motifs themselves. A single glaze can be an effective treatment for a wall, leaving a broken surface as opposed to the flat, single-toned finish that results from a roller. If you apply several layers of glaze, the surface becomes richer and multi-toned. Brush marks disappear under each successive glaze coat, leaving a soft, gently textured surface. (For an alternative effect, in which individual brush strokes remain clearer, see Part Two, p. 48.) Here we show how colourwashing can be used on its own to stripe a wall. In two of our samples, the two glazes we use are the same colour. This enriches the first glaze and brings it down a tone. In the other two samples, the second glaze is a different but similar colour. This creates a more complex and subtle surface. If you opt to use a second colour which is from a different part of the spectrum than the first, you will not end up with such subtlety. However, this should not stop you from experimenting if you wish.

The wall you are to work on should be well prepared and white. Good-quality matt emulsions are ideal as a base. Cheaper emulsions usually have chalk or whiting as a pigment which makes them too absorbent, so the glaze cannot be moved around on them.

The colourwash dries quickly, so, if you are tackling a large surface, it is a good idea to have two people working together. The scumble in the colourwash mix helps to extend slightly the glaze's drying time, making it a little easier to manipulate. It also gives the glaze a slightly harder finish.

The recipes are for a wall approximately 5m² (54ft²).

BASIC RECIPE – BLUE ON BLUE COLOURWASHED STRIPES

INGREDIENTS   **See swatch captions. Colourants: artists' acrylic colours.**

EQUIPMENT   **Medium-textured paint roller plus tray / 1 or 2 large containers / 2 or 4 x 100mm (4in) decorators' brushes / rags / tape measure / straightedge / water-soluble crayon or chalk line / masking tape for delicate surfaces / till roll**

INSTRUCTIONS   1 Prepare the surface thoroughly. See pp. 24–7.
2 Use a medium-textured paint roller to apply two coats of matt white emulsion to the wall. You should be aiming to create a surface which is free of brush strokes but has a slight texture. Leave 4 hours to dry between coats, and 24 hours after the second coat to be sure of having a really hard surface ready for the next stage.
3 Mix up your glaze or glazes in one or more containers.
4 Load one of the decorators' brushes with glaze and apply

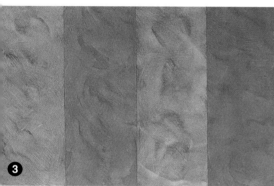

1 BLUE ON BLUE
On a base coat of 1 litre white emulsion, a mixture of 3tbsp white emulsion, ½tsp quincridone violet, 1tbsp ultramarine plus 150ml acrylic scumble and 500ml water will colourwash the wall twice.

3 DULL TURQUOISE GREEN ON BLUE
On 1 litre white emulsion, apply a first glaze of the swatch 1 colourwash, and a second glaze of 3tbsp white emulsion, 3tbsp cobalt blue, 2tsp yellow ochre, 100ml acrylic scumble and 400ml water.

it to a section of the wall. Brush it on in all directions in quick, curving, random strokes. Almost immediately, follow up with the clean, dry decorators' brush. Skim the second brush over the paint in all directions until you reach the point where the brush begins to drag and starts to lift the paint off rather than moving it around. Now you should work a little more firmly. Aim to soften all the brush strokes, but do not fret if some remain stronger than others. This is all part of the desired effect. The paint will be completely dry in only a matter of seconds.

5 Move quickly on to the next section of the wall and repeat the process. The second brush will become wet as you work, so you will need to dry it off frequently on a piece of rag. Repeat until you have completed the wall, then leave to dry for at least 4 hours.

6 Use the tape measure, straightedge and crayon to measure and mark out a series of 200mm (8in) stripes (see p. 35). Mask out alternate stripes with masking tape and till roll (see pp. 40–1). Take care when applying masking tape to the freshly painted areas. If possible, use a tape designed for delicate surfaces.

7 Use the decorators' brushes to apply the second glaze coat in the same manner as the first. Remove the masking and allow to dry (4 hours).

2 BEIGE ON BEIGE
Again on a base coat of 1 litre white emulsion, a mixture of 7½tbsp white and 3tbsp raw sienna mixed with 150ml acrylic scumble and 600ml water will be sufficient to colourwash the wall twice.

4 BROWN ON BEIGE
Again on 1 litre white emulsion, apply a first glaze of swatch 2 colourwash, and a second glaze of 2tbsp white emulsion, 4tbsp burnt sienna, 1½tsp dioxazine purple, 100ml acrylic scumble and 400ml water.

DRY-BRUSHED PANELS

Dry brushing is similar in many ways to colourwashing, but the overall effect is softer. Its real practical advantage in decorative contexts is that because the brush is not fully loaded with paint, runs, splashes, dribbles and seepage beneath masking tape are not usually a problem. The technique of dry brushing, however, requires some vigour, so we normally only apply a single coat, and we also work in smallish, contained areas. Here, we show that dividing a wall into panels of colour not only gives you a means to manage the technique, but also provides a discreet and easy-to-achieve design for a wall. We have used it on walls of random stripes too; the stripes were multiples of 50mm (2in) wide, with three colours applied in an ordered sequence.

As with colourwashing, your base coat should be good-quality white emulsion. Our standard recipe for dry brushing in Parts Three and Four is 1 part colour : 1 part acrylic scumble : 2 parts water, but it can be varied by using less or no water. Dark colours require the most water to lighten them, whereas pale colours work better with less. You should also take into account the quality of your paint. If it is thin and watery to begin with, then you will have to reduce the amount of water. Check the consistency by doing a trial run on an offcut of plasterboard. (See also Part Two, p. 58, where more water is used.) These recipes are for a wall approximately 6m² (65ft²).

BASIC RECIPE – EMERALD GREEN DRY-BRUSHED PANELS

INGREDIENTS

See swatch captions. Colourants: artists' acrylic colours

EQUIPMENT

Medium-textured paint roller plus tray / tape measure / straightedge / water-soluble crayon or chalk line / masking tape for delicate surfaces / till roll or clean paper / container / 1 x 100mm (4in) decorators' brush / ceramic tile

INSTRUCTIONS

1 Prepare the surface thoroughly. See pp. 24–7.
2 Use a medium-textured paint roller to apply two coats of matt white emulsion to the wall. You should be aiming to create a surface which is free of brush strokes but has a slight texture. Allow 4 hours to dry between coats, and 24 hours after the second coat.
3 Using the tape measure, straightedge and crayon, mark the wall out into panels 2–4m² (22–43ft²). The exact size will be governed by the size of your wall. Using the masking tape, mask off as many alternate panels as possible, extending the width of the masking with till roll or clean paper (see pp. 40–1).
4 Mix up the glaze coat in the container, then dab the tips of the decorators' brush into the glaze. Only a little is needed.

❶ EMERALD GREEN
Over a base coat of 1 litre white emulsion, we applied an emerald green glaze made from 4tbsp phthalo-cyanine green and 3tbsp yellow ochre added to 120ml white emulsion. The yellow ochre takes some of the sharpness out of the green. The colour was mixed with 225ml acrylic scumble and 500ml water.

❷ TERRACOTTA
With the same base coat as swatch 1, we used a glaze made from 160ml ready-mixed emulsion (BS 04 E 53), to which we added 8tsp burnt sienna and 4tsp white. The burnt sienna helps give the colour a more antique look. The colour was mixed with 220ml acrylic scumble and 450ml water.

❸ DOVE GREY
The simplest recipe and the most subtle. On the same base coat as before, apply a glaze made from 200ml white emulsion and 1tbsp black artists' acrylic colour mixed with 215ml acrylic scumble and 450ml water.

Stipple the brush on the tile to distribute the paint evenly across the bristles. Starting at the top of a panel, brush the paint out in all directions. You can use a rubbing action as well. The paint will spread out into a softly textured layer with variations in tone. Do not overwork the glaze or you may start to rub it off.

5 Once you have used up the glaze on your brush, dip it into the glaze again, stipple it on the tile, and continue down the panel. You must work briskly in order to blend one section successfully with the next. As you proceed, you will see the wisdom of dividing the wall up into small, manageable areas.

6 Complete each of the masked-off panels in turn, then remove the masking tape. Leave to dry for 2 hours to ensure the glaze is not disturbed at the next stage.

7 Mask off another set of panels and repeat. Take care when applying masking tape to the freshly painted areas. If possible, use a tape designed for delicate surfaces. Remove the masking and allow to dry (2 hours).

Continue like this until all the panels have been completed. The soft chequerboard effect will appear as a result of slight variations in the colour and texture typical of this technique.

COMBED BORDERS

This involves dragging a purpose-made comb through wet paint to leave a pattern of ridges similar to the look of a woven fabric. The combs are usually sold in sets, giving a choice of three different-sized teeth in four or five widths of comb. You may be able to achieve similar effects with tile-cement spreaders or with home-made combs cut from plastic or card. These recipes will cover approximately 4m² (43ft²).

COMBING OVER COLOURWASHING

INGREDIENTS

See swatch captions. Colourants: artists' acrylic colours.

EQUIPMENT

Choose from the following:
Screw-top jars / paint roller plus tray / small paint kettle / 2 x 100mm (4in) decorators' brush / masking tape for delicate surfaces / till roll / 80–100mm (3–4in) wide broad-toothed comb / rag / wet and dry paper

INSTRUCTIONS

1 Prepare the surface thoroughly. See pp. 24–7.

2 Mix up the first colour – the background and combing colour – in a screw-top jar. Using the roller, paint on two coats , allowing 2–4 hours for each coat to dry.

3 Mix up the colourwash in another screw-top jar and use the two larger brushes to apply two coats (see pp. 124–5), allowing 2 hours between coats and overnight for the second coat to dry.

4 Using masking tape for delicate surfaces in conjunction with till roll, mask out the border (see pp. 40–1). If the band is going to turn a corner, as here, mitre the corner with masking tape as well.

5 Using a smaller brush, apply a liberal amount of the first colour along a 1–2m (3–6ft) section of the border. Do not skimp. It must be thick enough for the comb to leave it standing up in ridges.

6 Without hesitation, drag the comb across the wet paint at

❶ WISTERIA OVER PEA GREEN
Here the first colour is 500ml white emulsion mixed with 1tbsp ultramarine. The colourwash is 2tbsp white emulsion, 4tbsp cadmium yellow and 2tsp raw umber, mixed with 100ml scumble and 400ml water.

❷ LINEN OVER HYACINTH
The first colour is 500ml white emulsion with 5tsp raw umber. The colourwash is 4tbsp white emulsion, and 2tsp each ultramarine and dioxazine purple, mixed with 5½tbsp acrylic scumble and 320ml water.

right angles to the masking tape. Do not stop until you reach the opposite edge of the border. As you pull the comb across, vary the pattern by increasing and decreasing the pressure on it or by allowing it to wander in gentle wavy lines. Reposition the comb in the adjacent area of wet paint, slightly overlapping the first, and pull it across the paint once more. You will occasionally need to wipe excess paint from the comb with a damp rag.

7 Repeat along the border until you reach the end of a band, as it is not easy to join wet combing to dry. Remove any masking tape and leave to dry thoroughly. As the paint is thick, this may take longer than the normal recommended time of 4 hours.

8 Mask the other sides of the mitres, and repeat the combing on the remaining sides.

9 Remove the masking along the edges of the border to reveal a crisply edged border with a ribbed finish.

COMBING UNDER COLOURWASHING

Combing under colourwashing makes the combed band look more subtle. It is carried out in exactly the same manner as described above, except that the combing is done first and the colourwashing second. After colourwashing, rub the combed ridges over very lightly with wet and dry paper dipped in water. This will reveal their colour.

❶ WISTERIA UNDER DANDELION YELLOW The background and combing colour consists of 500ml white emulsion mixed with 1tbsp ultramarine. The colourwash is 4tbsp white emulsion, 4tsp yellow ochre and 2tsp each phthalocyanine green and payne's grey, mixed with 6tbsp scumble and 360ml water.

❷ LINEN UNDER CLEMATIS The background and combing colour is again 500ml white emulsion with 5tsp raw umber, as in swatch 2 of combing over colourwashing, while the colourwash consists of 2tbsp each dioxazine purple, quinacridone red and white emulsion, mixed with 6tbsp acrylic scumble and 270ml water.

❶

❷

SPONGED PANELS

More ideas for panels: two-colour bands for a border design and simple repeating motifs. Experiment with the range of sponges available; each gives a different finish. Here we use standard household sponges. Try varying the amount of paint applied as well to achieve anything from an opaque finish to an open texture which reveals the colour below. (See Part Two, p. 52, for a finish that combines Sponging off and on.)

SPONGING ON

Sponging on is our standard method of applying paint for stencilling. It is also a quick and easy way of giving a texture to a surface, for instance the granular texture on our counter front on pp. 184–7. This recipe will cover an area approximately 5m² (54ft²).

INGREDIENTS

See swatch captions. Colourants: artists' acrylic colours.

EQUIPMENT

Paint roller plus tray / 3 household sponges / scissors / 3 screw-top jars / 3 large plates / tape measure / masking tape for delicate surfaces / till roll

INSTRUCTIONS

1 Prepare the surface thoroughly. See pp. 24–7.

2 Use the roller to apply two coats of white emulsion, allowing each coat to dry (4 hours).

3 Squared-off sponges can leave lines in the paint, so trim them into a more rounded shape with scissors.

4 Mix up each of the sponging colours in a screw-top jar and spoon some of the first colour onto a plate. Dip your sponge into it, then pat it up and down for a moment to spread the paint evenly across the surface of the sponge. If you feel you have too much on your sponge, pat it on the plate a little longer. To create the lightly textured effect that is required here, the holes in the sponge should not be filled with paint.

5 Use a light dabbing motion to sponge the paint on. Try to vary the action as you work, or you may find that you are building up a pattern that is too repetitious. Complete the sponging in this manner, reloading your sponge with paint at regular intervals. Allow to dry (2–4 hours).

6 Use masking tape and till roll to mask off a 200mm (8in) wide band (see pp. 40–1). Sponge in the same way with the second sponging colour. Remove the masking and allow to dry (2–4 hours).

7 Mask off the second band in the same way, and sponge in the third colour. Remove the masking and allow to dry. The final effect is similar in appearance to a woven fabric such as gingham or madras cotton.

❶ BLUE GREEN AND DARK GREY OVER CREAMY YELLOW
Here the base coat is 1 litre white emulsion, with a first sponged coat of 500ml white emulsion mixed with 2tsp cadmium yellow, 2tsp yellow ochre and 1tsp neutral grey. The second sponged coat is 8tsp white emulsion with 6tbsp black and 2tbsp burnt umber. The third sponged coat is 5½tbsp white emulsion, 5½tbsp cobalt blue and 4tsp yellow ochre.

❷ BLUE GREY AND PEACH OVER LILAC
With the same base coat as in swatch 1, the first sponged coat is 450ml white emulsion mixed with 1tbsp neutral grey and 2tsp dioxazine purple. The second sponged coat is 150ml white emulsion mixed with 2tbsp ultramarine, while the third is 5tbsp white emulsion mixed with 100ml yellow ochre and 1tbsp naphthol red.

SPONGING OFF

This technique is an essential part of the stone finishes on pp. 94–5; it also provided the backgrounds to the tables on pp. 212–15, and gave texture to the stripe on pp. 144–6. On a small scale, sponging off will also modify the texture of a motif: use a clean, damp sponge on the freshly painted surface.

In essence, with sponging off, paint is applied, then some is lifted off with a wet or damp sponge. If you splash, spray or sprinkle water onto the paint as it dries, it will soften in those places and this paint will lift off more readily. Open, more vigorously textured sponging off requires a lot of water, so can only be carried out successfully on a horizontal surface. On walls, use plant misters and wet sponges.

For an area such as the top of a small table, you will only need about two or three tablespoons of colour, depending on the texture you are aiming for. This recipe will cover an area approximately 3m² (32ft²).

INGREDIENTS — See swatch captions (over). Colourants: artists' acrylic colours.

EQUIPMENT — Paint roller plus tray / 2 large plates / 1 x 80mm (3in) decorators' brush / bowl of water / plant mister (optional) / 2 or 3 household sponges / paper / scissors / repositionable spray adhesive

GRAINED FLOOR DESIGN

This is a development of the graining design illustrated on the previous page, but in it we make use of more subdued colour schemes. You will need to start with a smooth floor, one made of blockboard for example. We envisaged using the design to cover a floor from wall to wall, although you could easily adapt it to make a border for a floor or even an all-over design for a table top.

BASIC RECIPE – TURQUOISE AND AUBERGINE

PREPARATION

Prepare the surface thoroughly. See pp. 24–7.

INGREDIENTS

For a floor approximately 5m² (54ft²)
First colour ▶ 1.2 litres white vinyl matt emulsion / 300ml neutral grey artists' acrylic colour / 1tbsp phthalocyanine green artists' acrylic colour
Second colour ▶ 600ml raw umber artists' acrylic colour / 225ml neutral grey artists' acrylic colour / 225ml dioxazine purple artists' acrylic colour
Protective coat ▶ 1.5 litres matt acrylic floor varnish

EQUIPMENT

2 containers / 2 paint rollers plus trays / card / metal ruler / pencil / scalpel / cutting mat / water-soluble crayon / chalk line / 50mm (2in) masking tape / 60mm (2½in) till roll / scissors / repositionable spray adhesive / paper / masking tape for delicate surfaces / 1 x 50mm (2in) decorators' brush / graining rocker / 1 x 100mm (4in) varnish brush or roller

INSTRUCTIONS
Background

Mix up the first colour in a container and paint the floor with two coats using the roller. Allow 2–4 hours between coats, and leave overnight after the second coat.

Squares

1 Use the scalpel to cut a 60mm (2½in) square hole at the centre of a 300mm (12in) square piece of card. Cut a second piece of card 90 x 300mm (3½ x 12in). With the aid of these templates, the crayon and a chalk line, mark out a grid of 300mm (12in) squares separated by 90mm (3½in) spaces across the whole floor. Use the 50mm (2in) masking tape to mask out the spaces (see pp. 40–1).
2 Mix up the second colour in another container, and use a roller to paint the squares with two coats of this colour, allowing 4 hours for each coat to dry.
3 Cut the till roll into as many squares as you have painted. Spray one side of each of these with adhesive and set them at the centre of each painted square using the square cardboard template as a guide.

GRAINED FLOOR DESIGN

❶ TURQUOISE AND AUBERGINE
The basic recipe.

❷ CREAM AND SLATE BLUE
The first colour is 1200ml white, 80ml hansa yellow light and 80ml raw umber. The second colour is 600ml cobalt blue, 200ml mars black and 200ml white.

4 Cut plenty of 300mm (12in) squares of paper each into four triangles.

5 Using the masking tape for delicate surfaces in conjunction with the paper triangles, mask off completely along the diagonals, opposite sections of each square, leaving the other two sections exposed. Hold down the bottom edge of the paper triangles with another piece of masking tape.

❸ BRONZE AND SLATE BLUE
The first colour is a ready-mixed emulsion – BS 06 D 43. The square is painted in a mix of 900ml white and 150ml neutral grey, while the graining colour is 1 litre of the second colour from swatch 2.

Graining

1 Using the decorators' brush and the first colour, paint in the two exposed sections fairly thickly. Immediately, drag the rocker across the wet paint to create the graining pattern (see p. 133). Remove the paper triangles and the masking tape and allow to dry (at least 4 hours).

2 Mask out for the remaining two sections of each square and repeat step 1 above, then very carefully remove all the masking. Leave to harden (1–2 days).

Protective coat

Using the varnish brush and following the manufacturers' instructions, apply at least three coats of varnish.

STAMPED MOTIFS

Like stencils, rubber stamps are an effective way of reproducing a motif, but they are much quicker to use, producing a soft, varied texture which suits both contemporary and more traditional interiors. You can buy ready-made rubber stamps, but it is not difficult to make your own (see p. 38). Acrylic paint is ideal for stamping. If the stamp is small, press it onto a layer of paint rolled out on a ceramic tile. For larger stamps, apply the paint to the stamp with the roller (see p. 39). Practise stamping on a scrap of paper to discover how much paint you need and how much pressure to apply. The following recipes will cover approximately 4m² (43ft²).

INGREDIENTS

See swatch captions. Colourants: artists' acrylic colour.

EQUIPMENT

Choose from the following:
Container / paint roller plus tray / tape measure / water-soluble crayon / string / card (optional) / 150 x 250mm (6 x 10in) foam-rubber mat / 150 x 250mm (6 x 10in) foam-core or marine-ply backing board / contact adhesive / 2 screw-top jars / 2 ceramic tiles / small paint roller / bowl of water / 1 or 2 sponges / felt-tip pen / tracing paper / pencil / paper / scalpel / cloth

This design uses one square stamp twice to produce a motif with a shadow of itself behind. It could be stamped at random but, as with the stencilling (see pp. 156–7), we prefer a more orderly arrangement.

INSTRUCTIONS

1 Prepare the surface thoroughly (see pp. 24–7) and use the roller to paint on two coats of background colour, allowing 2–4 hours for each coat to dry.
2 Measure and mark out the layout, using string as a guide for each of the horizontal lines of squares (see p. 35).
3 Mark out the spacing between each square with the crayon or cut a piece of card to the width of the space required and use this to guide you as you proceed.
4 Make a 40mm (1½in) square stamp of foam rubber glued to a backing board of the same dimensions (see p. 38).

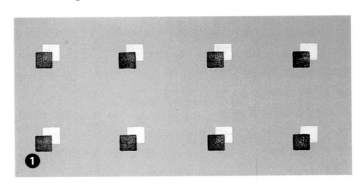

❶ **PALE SHADOWS**
The background is 200ml white emulsion mixed with 300ml yellow ochre. The first stamp colour is ¼tsp payne's grey with 50ml white emulsion and the second is 50ml payne's grey. These will each print approximately 100 squares.

5 Mix up the two colours and spoon some of the first onto a tile. Roller out a generous, even layer and press your stamp into it. Stamp lines of squares along and up the wall. Clean the stamp by patting it up and down in a little water or on a wet sponge, then gently dry it with a cloth.

6 Press the stamp into a little of the second colour on a tile. The second motif overlaps the first, a little way below and to the left of it. To get it in the right place each time, mark a line on the upper and right-hand edges of the backing board and align these with the left-hand side and lower edge of the first squares each time you print.

AN ORNATE STAMP

This stamp is in two sections but there is no reason why any number of sections should not be used, depending on your patience and ingenuity. It has been designed to make a border, but it could be used for an all-over pattern.

INSTRUCTIONS

1 Follow the instructions for simple stamping.

2 Measure for the lower edge of the border and stretch a string tautly along this line.

3 Trace the motif on p. 216, enlarge it to 220mm (8½in) and cut out the two sections. Arrange them on the foam-rubber and use as templates (see p. 38). It will print as a mirror-image, so ensure that its two sections are the right way round. Draw a line on the reverse of the backing board opposite the tip of the motif to help with lining up.

4 Mix the stamping colour and spoon some onto a tile. Roll it out with a small roller, then roller over the stamp to deposit an even film of paint on it. Place it in position, lining up its bottom edge with the string, then press firmly.

5 Repeat to complete the border. As there is no spacing between motifs, when you print, place the end of the stamp alongside the end of the previous motif.

2 PAYNE'S GREY ON PALE OCHRE This background is the same as that used for the simple stamp and the stamp colour is again 50ml payne's grey, but this amount will only print 50 of these larger motifs.

6 You may come up against an obstruction such as a window, door or corner where you will not be able to stamp a complete motif. If the empty spaces are very small and unobtrusive, you can simply leave them as they are. If you have finished the rest of your border and only have one or two more spaces to fill, you can cut the stamp down to make a motif that will fit the spaces. This will be easy to do if you have used a foam-core backing board. If you need a lot more motifs, stamp several prints onto paper and cut them out to make paper stencils which you only use once. Bend the paper stencil into corners or cut it to fit up to doors or windows, then sponge on the paint, mimicking the texture of the design as a whole.

A TWO-STAMP DESIGN

Here we employ the already-prepared simple stamp and ornate stamp to make a third, more elaborate design which we use as a border.

INSTRUCTIONS

1 Follow the instructions for simple stamping.
2 Use a tape measure to measure out two lines spaced 220mm (8½in) apart. Stretch strings tautly along these lines.
3 Follow step 5 of Simple stamping, printing the squares at 100mm (4in) intervals inside the two lines. Note how the squares of the lower line are staggered to the right by the width of one square.
4 Spoon a little of the second colour onto a tile, roller it out and roller it over the second stamp. Print this vertically between the squares, using the string and the squares to guide you. Ensure that the top and bottom points of the second stamp fall exactly between two squares. You should not need any complex marking out, providing you have cut the backing board of the second stamp square and its stamp is positioned centrally on it.

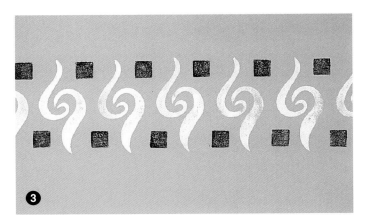

❸

❸ PALE GREY AND PAYNE'S GREY
Again, the background colour is the same as that already used, and the first and second stamp colours are as before.

MOSAIC BORDER DESIGN

Painting a mosaic might seem a time-consuming business at first glance, but using a set of foam-rubber stamps can speed things up no end. We have confined this design to a border on a floor, but if you are more ambitious, you could cover the whole floor in a similar manner. With careful planning you can make your border go around corners and into alcoves, or you could set it as a rectangle or square regardless of the shape of your room. You could also of course happily run this border along a wall.

If you apply the border to a floor, the smoother and flatter the floor, the easier it will be to print. We have used blockboard as our base. This takes a water-based wood stain very well and the stain can subsequently be painted over without any problem using acrylic paints. If you like the idea of the mosaic but have a different floor surface, then alter the background accordingly. Chipboard, for example, could be given a stone finish (as for the *Rose des Vents* on pp. 166–7). Floorboards might seem an unlikely site for a mosaic but if you have new, featureless boards, a mosaic may just prove to be the quirky idea which will bring them to life.

BASIC RECIPE – BLACK AND WHITE ON UMBER

PREPARATION   Prepare the surface thoroughly. See pp. 24–7.

INGREDIENTS   *For a border approximately 10m (33ft) long*
Background ▶ umber water-based floor stain. See manufacturers' instructions for quantity required for your floor.
Base coat ▶ 300ml white vinyl matt emulsion / 2tbsp raw umber artists' acrylic colour
First mosaic colour ▶ 150ml white artists' acrylic colour
Second mosaic colour ▶ 3tbsp black artists' acrylic colour / 1tbsp phthalocyanine blue artists' acrylic colour / 2tsp white artists' acrylic colour
Protective coat ▶ acrylic floor varnish. See manufacturers' instructions for quantity required for your floor.

EQUIPMENT   1 x 100mm (4in) decorators' brush / medium-grade sandpaper / tape measure / ruler / graph paper / pencil / chalk line or string / masking tape / till roll / container / 3 small paint rollers / 1 paint tray / 4 foam-core or marine-ply backing boards: 2 of 180 x 180mm (7 x 7in); 1 of 60 x 60mm (2½ x 2½in); 1 of 60 x 40 x 40mm (2½ x 1½ x 1½in) / 140 x 200mm (5½ x 8in) foam-rubber mat / scalpel / cutting mat / small tube contact adhesive / 2 screw-top jars / 3 ceramic tiles / newspaper / 1 x 100mm (4in) varnish brush

MOSAIC BORDER DESIGN

INSTRUCTIONS

Background

Using the decorators' brush and following the manufacturers' instructions, give the floor one or two coats of stain as required. Use the sandpaper to sand lightly after applying each coat.

Border

The 180mm (7in) wide border consists of two alternating 180mm (7in) square motifs. Plan the position of your border on the floor. In a perfect world, each length of border would divide exactly into an odd number of squares, but the chances of this are slim. With the aid of graph paper and a little forethought, though, you can plan for the best possible layout. If you are unable to fit in all the squares exactly, it will not be too serious a problem. When printing, you will be starting from a corner and working along a side to its midpoint, which is where the problem will be resolved (see Printing, step 2 below).

Set out the border with a chalk line or string and mask the surrounding area with tape and till roll (see pp. 35 and 40–1).

Base coat

Mix up the base coat colour in the large container and apply the paint to the border using a small roller. Some of this base coat will show through between the mosaics as grout, so ensure a good coverage. Give it two coats if necessary.

Stamps

1 Make up the four individual stamps used in the design (see p. 38). The two main stamps – the crosses – are 180mm (7in) square. For these, draw a grid of 20mm (¾in) squares on the first 180 x 180mm (7 x 7in) backing board. Draw a similar grid, but this time set out on the diagonal, on the second 180 x 180mm (7 x 7in) board. Cut the foam mat up into 17mm (⅝in) squares and stick these with contact adhesive to the backing boards to form the two crosses. You will also need a few small triangular pieces of foam to complete the diagonally placed cross.

2 Using the small square backing board and the triangular piece of board, make up the other two stamps in exactly the same way.

Printing

1 Mix up the first and second mosaic colours in the screw-top jars. To print the border, begin with the two crosses. Place a spoonful or two of the first mosaic colour on a tile, then transfer some to the stamp with a roller. Test the stamp out before you start. This will let you see if the design is printing well, allow you to gauge how much paint to roller on and how much pressure to apply. You will need to press

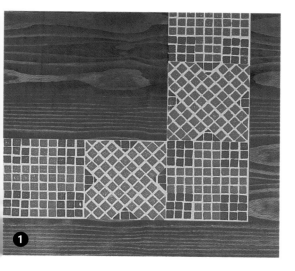

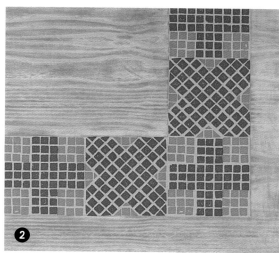

❶ GREEN AND TERRACOTTA ON MAHOGANY
Here we used a more traditional wood colouring – in this case a mahogany stain – for the background. The base coat is as for the basic recipe. The red mosaic is mixed from 3tbsp magenta, 3tbsp mars red and 2tbsp white, while the green mosaic is made using 4tsp white, 4tsp phthalocyanine green and 1tsp payne's grey.

the stamp down firmly, but not so hard that paint squeezes out sideways.

Once you are confident that you have the knack, begin at a corner, printing alternate crosses as you go. As you approach the centre of the side, switch to the opposite corner and work along from there, starting with the same cross as before.

2 If you are unable to finish the line with a complete cross, then ensure that the last print on either side of the centre is of the same pattern.

You now have to fill the remaining space with a motif which may be larger or smaller than a complete cross. To do this, place a sheet of newspaper along a line which is half a grout width beyond the centre line. The newspaper will act as a mask and will not allow you to print beyond this centre line. Print the next cross butted up to the last, but overlapping the newspaper. Remove the newspaper and allow this print to dry for 5–10 minutes.

3 Place a fresh sheet of paper over this last print and again along a line half a grout width beyond the centre line. Print the motif in the remaining space. Remove the paper to reveal a symmetrical centre motif.

Alternatively, you could design a completely new stamp for this space –– for example, a series of vertical stripes or a stamp with your initials.

4 Complete the design in the same way with the second mosaic colour and the two remaining stamps.

Protective coat

Leave to dry for at least 24 hours. Then, using the varnish brush, apply a minimum of three coats of varnish according to the manufacturers' instructions.

❷ BLUE AND OCHRE ON PALE BLUE
The ready-mixed floor stain is in one of the brighter colours that are now available and has been used as a background for a border with a more Mediterranean colouring. For the blue, we mixed 4tbsp cobalt blue with 4tbsp white and 1tsp payne's grey. The contrasting mosaics are in 3–4tbsp yellow ochre. The base coat is again as for the basic recipe.

OAK-LEAF BORDER DESIGN

Borders are a classic way of dividing up walls. They may be used at dado-height to divide a wall into an upper and a lower section or, as here, around a panel to create a frame. In this project, we have made an oak-leaf stamp from a piece of foam rubber and used it to stamp a border that marks the dividing line between an area of colourwashing and one of flat painting.

BASIC RECIPE – LINEN, RASPBERRY AND SALMON

PREPARATION   **Prepare the surface thoroughly. See pp. 24–7.**

INGREDIENTS   *For a wall 4–5m² (43–54ft²) with an 8m (26ft) border*
Colourwash ▸ 5tsp naphthol red artists' acrylic colour / 5tsp white artists' acrylic colour / 10tsp acrylic scumble / water in the ratio 1 part colour : 1 part scumble : 4 parts water
Flat paint ▸ 400ml white vinyl matt emulsion / 120ml yellow ochre artists' acrylic colour / 4tsp payne's grey artists' acrylic colour
Leaf motif ▸ 1tbsp white artists' acrylic colour / 2tsp mars red artists' acrylic colour

EQUIPMENT   **Tape measure / chalk line and/or spirit level / water-soluble crayon / 2 large containers / 2 x 120mm (5in) decorators' brushes / masking tape for delicate surfaces / paint roller plus tray / tracing paper / pencil / foam-rubber mat / scissors or scalpel / cutting mat / foam-core or marine-ply backing board / small tube contact adhesive / screw-top jar / ceramic tile / small paint roller**

INSTRUCTIONS
Layout   Plan the layout of your design (see p. 34) and mark the line between the colourwashed and the flat-painted areas using a water-soluble crayon.

Background   **1** Mix the colourwash in one of the large containers and brush it on (see pp. 124–5), extending it to just beyond the crayon line. Allow to dry thoroughly for at least 4 hours.
2 If the crayon line is no longer visible, mark it out again, then mask off the colourwashed area with masking tape (see p. 40).
3 Mix the flat paint colour in the other container and apply it evenly using the roller. Apply a minimum of two coats in order to achieve a flat matt surface, allowing 4 hours between coats. Remove the masking tape and allow to dry (4 hours).

Stamp   **1** Meanwhile, trace the motif on p. 216 and use it to make the stamp (see pp. 38–9).
2 In our design the leaf is stamped at 50mm (2in) intervals

❶ LINEN, RASPBERRY AND SALMON
The basic recipe.

❷ MIDNIGHT, JASMINE AND BLUE GREY
Here the colourwash is made from 10tsp hansa yellow light mixed with a scant ⅛tsp payne's grey, 10tsp acrylic scumble and water in the correct ratio. The flat colour consists of 400ml black emulsion, 120ml phthalocyanine blue and 16tsp white emulsion. The motif colour is made with 1tbsp white mixed with ½tsp payne's grey and a scant ¼tsp each cobalt blue and yellow ochre.

❸ FLAME, SLATE AND JASMINE
The colourwash here is made from 2tbsp payne's grey, 1tbsp white, 3tbsp acrylic scumble and water in the correct ratio. The flat paint is a mixture of 500ml ready-mixed emulsion – BS 04 E 53 – and 4tsp naphthol red. The motif is stamped with 5tbsp hansa yellow light and ⅛tsp payne's grey.

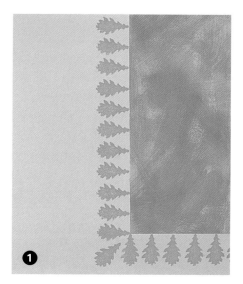

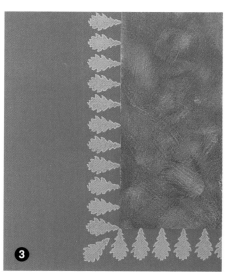

around the area of colourwashing. Mark out the positions of the leaf using the water-soluble crayon.

3 Mix the white and mars red artists' acrylic colours in the screw-top jar to make the leaf colour and spoon a little of it onto the ceramic tile. Spread it out with the small roller, then press the stamp into the paint to coat the stamp with an even layer of the colour (see p. 39).

4 Press the stamp down firmly onto the flat-painted section of wall, ensuring that the stamp is at right angles to the line and that the stalk of the leaf is on one of your crayon marks.

5 Continue along the line, recharging the stamp with paint to print each motif.

6 If you are working on a panel design, the corners will appear empty, so you must stamp an extra leaf here. For this extra leaf, position the stamp so that the outer tips of its leaf line up to form a right angle at the corner.

❹ JASMINE, EMERALD AND TERRACOTTA
Here the colourwash is 5tsp white blended with 2½tsp yellow ochre and 2½tsp phthalocyanine green, together with 10tsp acrylic scumble and water in the correct ratio. The flat paint is 500ml ready-mixed emulsion – BS 10 E 53 – and the motif is stamped using 1tbsp mars red.

SIMPLE BORDER DESIGN

You could paint this border single-handed, but it would be quicker and more fun to enlist the help of a friend. This will also ensure that, as you proceed along the stripe, you maintain a wet edge as one of you paints and sprays while the other follows up with the sponge to create the texture. If you want to pause, you should only do so at a corner or at a fixture such as a door. If you can foresee that you will have to pause part-way along a wall, then before you start, divide the border into equal lengths using masking tape. You should then complete alternate sections, taking your breaks when a section is painted. When you are ready to start again, mask off the painted sections and fill in the others. The joins between the sections will show, but they will be quite smart and at predetermined intervals.

BASIC RECIPE – BOTTLE GREEN WITH COPPER

PREPARATION **Prepare the surface thoroughly. See pp. 24–7.**

INGREDIENTS *For a wall 4–5m² (43–54ft²) with a border 5m x 100mm (16ft x 4in)*
Background colour ▶ 500ml white vinyl matt emulsion / 1tsp payne's grey artists' acrylic colour / 1tsp raw umber artists' acrylic colour / 1tsp ultramarine artists' acrylic colour
Stripe ▶ 2tsp phthalocyanine green artists' acrylic colour / 2tsp black artists' acrylic colour / 2tsp white vinyl matt emulsion
Motif ▶ 20ml iridescent copper artists' acrylic colour

EQUIPMENT **Container / paint roller plus tray / tape measure / water-soluble crayon / string / masking tape for delicate surfaces / newspaper / screw-top jar / 1 x 50mm (2in) decorators' brush / plant mister / water / 2 household sponges / tracing paper / pencil / flat square eraser / scalpel / ceramic tile / small paint roller**

INSTRUCTIONS
Background

Mix up the background colour in the container. Use the roller to apply two or three coats to the wall, allowing 4 hours for each coat to dry, then leave the surface to harden off thoroughly – several days if possible.

Layout

1 Having decided on the height you would like for the top edge of your border, in one corner of the room measure up from the floor or down from the ceiling to this height (see p. 35). Mark lightly on the wall with water-soluble crayon. Repeat in the next corner. Stretch a string between these two points, attaching it with masking tape.
2 Stand back and consider this line. Once you are satisfied, fix masking tape both along the string line and 100mm (4in) below it to mark the lower edge of the border. Repeat on

❶ BOTTLE GREEN WITH COPPER
The basic recipe.

❷ PEWTER WITH FLAX
Here the background colour is the same as in the basic recipe, while the stripe is painted with 60ml iridescent pewter and the motif is stamped with a mixture of 5tsp white emulsion, 1½tsp yellow ochre and 4tsp payne's grey. The iridescent paint used here for the stripe will take longer to dry than the paint used in the basic recipe. You should wait about 5 minutes instead of 2 or 3, before spraying with water.

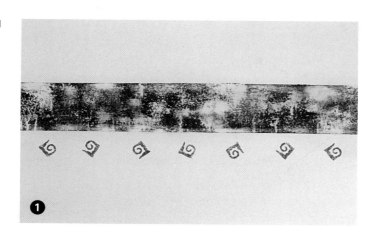

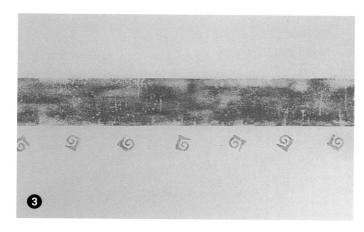

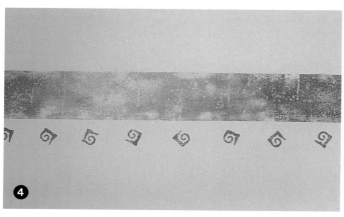

❸ DUSTY MAUVE WITH OLD GOLD
Here the background colour is a mixture of 500ml white emulsion, 150ml yellow ochre and 5tsp payne's grey. The stripe is painted with 5tsp white emulsion mixed with ½tsp dioxazine purple and 2tsp payne's grey. The motif is stamped first using 20ml purple, then with 20ml iridescent gold. Leave the purple paint to dry before you overstamp.

❹ COPPER WITH DUSTY MAUVE
The background colour is the same as in swatch 3, with the stripe painted in 60ml iridescent copper. The motif uses the purple of the motif of swatch 3. As in swatch 2, the iridescent paint used here for the stripe will take longer to dry than the paint used in the basic recipe.

each of the walls to be painted. To protect the walls during the next stages, extend the masked-off area with the addition of newspaper above and below the lines of tape.

Stripe

1 Mix the stripe colour in the screw-top jar and brush it on to a length of about 1m (3ft) between the lines of tape. Leave to dry for 2–3 minutes.

2 Spray the painted area with water from a plant mister and leave again for 2–3 minutes.

3 Use a sponge to dab at the wet surface. Where the water has landed on or run down the surface, the paint will be soft and the sponge will start to lift it off, leaving a textured effect (see pp. 131–2).

4 Repeat the spray / wait / dab (and perhaps rub and wipe) procedure until you have achieved the effect you want.

5 Paint the next 1m (3ft) or so of stripe, joining it gently to the completed section. Repeat the texturing technique with the spray and sponge. This will also allow you to make invisible joins between the sections.

6 As you proceed along the wall, take off the masking tape and remove any colour that has seeped behind the tape using a clean, damp sponge. If any of it has dried, wipe off what you can and touch up with the background colour.

Motif

1 Trace the design on p. 216 and use it to make the spiral motif rubber stamp (see p. 38).

2 Stretch a string, as in Layout, step 1 above, 25mm (1in) below the stripe.

3 Spoon a little of the motif paint onto a large ceramic tile, roll the paint out using the small roller and press the stamp into it, just as you would a stamp into an ink pad (see p. 39). Stamp the spiral motif along the string line, turning it a little each time as you progress to give the impression that it is spinning along. The spacing between motifs is not so critical that it cannot be judged by eye alone.

STIPPLED PANEL DESIGN

Earlier in Part Three, we showed that techniques such as dry brushing and colourwashing, normally used to create all-over texture, can be applied in blocks or stripes. Stippling can be similarly organized. This not only makes it more manageable when using water-based paints, which dry quickly, but also visually breaks up the surface with a restrained geometric design. (See Part Two, p. 56, for oil-based stippling.)

BASIC RECIPE – COBALT BLUE ON MARS RED

PREPARATION

Prepare the surface thoroughly. See pp. 24–7.

INGREDIENTS

To cover approximately 4m² (43ft²)
Base coat ▶ 300ml white vinyl matt emulsion
Stipple coat ▶ 2tsp mars red artists' acrylic colour / 2tsp yellow ochre artists' acrylic colour / 200ml acrylic scumble / water in the ratio 1 part colour : 10 parts scumble : 3 parts water
Motif ▶ 1tsp cobalt blue artists' acrylic colour / 1tsp mars red artists' acrylic colour

EQUIPMENT

1 x 200mm (8in) medium-textured paint roller plus tray / tape measure / plumb line and/or spirit level / water-soluble crayon / masking tape for delicate surfaces / large container / 1 x 150mm (6in) decorators' brush / brush for stippling / household sponge / tracing paper / pencil / flat square eraser / scalpel / ceramic tile

INSTRUCTIONS
Base coats

Use the roller to paint the wall with one or two coats of white emulsion. This should leave it opaque white with a slight orange-peel texture. Allow 4 hours to dry between coats, and at least 24 hours before the next stage.

Stipple coat

1 Divide the wall into rectangular or square blocks, marking them out using the tape measure, plumb line and/or spirit level and the water-soluble crayon (see p. 35). Each block should be no bigger than 400mm (16in) along each side. Mask off alternate blocks with masking tape.

2 Mix the stipple coat in the large container. Before applying it to the wall, bear in mind the short amount of time you will have to work when using water-based paint. We adopt two strategies to get round this difficulty. The first is to work in small sections as explained above. The second is for two people to work in unison. The first worker spreads out the paint with the decorators' brush, while the second follows with the stippling brush. The aim is to maintain a wet edge at all times. Once the paint dries it will be impossible to stipple it off and create the distinctive soft texture. So, using the

STIPPLED PANEL DESIGN

decorators' brush, apply the glaze in a thin layer to one of the panels. Immediately taking up the other clean, dry brush, dab it all over the wet glaze. Continue until all the brush marks have disappeared and are replaced with an even, all-over, grainy texture.

3 Once you have stippled alternate squares, remove the masking tape. Allow to dry (3–4 hours).

4 Mask out the remaining blocks and stipple them in the same way. To achieve the darker tone and create a gentle chequerboard pattern, these blocks were stippled twice, leaving half an hour between coats.

❶ COBALT BLUE ON MARS RED
The basic recipe. The red oxide is as strong as the blue, and, being almost the same tone, begins to resonate with it. Such colour contrasts can be striking without losing any of their elegance.

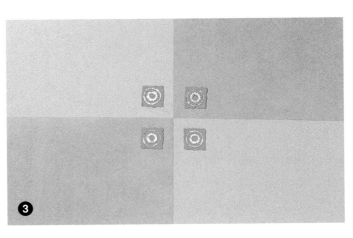

❷ MARS RED ON GREEN
Here the motif is 1tsp mars red stamped with phthalocyanine green. The stipple is made from 2tsp white, 2tsp raw umber and 1tsp phthalocyanine green mixed with 250ml scumble and water in ratio.

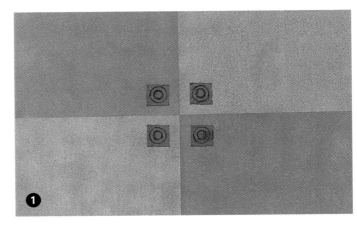

❸ YELLOW OCHRE ON PALE BLUE
To make the cool stipple colour, dilute 4tsp white, 1tsp cobalt and ½tsp raw umber with scumble and water as before. Here the motif background is 1tsp yellow ochre stamped with 1tsp white.

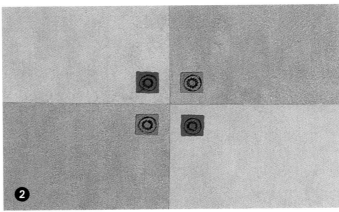

THE MOTIFS
In our swatches we have gone a step further and decorated the corners of the blocks with a simple motif. We would not decorate every set of four squares in this way. In fact, not decorating them all would look far more effective. You could, for example, dot groups of four around a room, or arrange them at random, or arrange them at any height along a wall to form a border.

To create the four squares, lay a grid of torn masking tape (see p. 41), sponge on the background colour and leave to dry. Trace the design on p. 216 and make the rubber stamp (see p. 38). Roll out a little of the motif paint on a tile, press the stamp into it and apply (see p. 39).

The principle of resists is quite simple. Apply a design in a resist to a background, then paint over it and the surrounding area. The resist will prevent this layer of paint from adhering. Once it is dry, remove the resist together with the paint, to reveal the design in the background colour. The following recipes will cover approximately 4m² (43ft²).

PAINTED-WAX RESIST

INGREDIENTS See swatch captions. Colourants: artists' acrylic colours.

EQUIPMENT 2 containers / 2 x 75mm (3in) decorators' brushes / tracing paper / pencil / paper / chalk / jar or tin / saucepan / plate warmer (optional) / small artists' fitch or other small artists' brush / spatula / wet and dry paper (optional)

INSTRUCTIONS

1 Prepare the surface thoroughly (see pp. 24–7), and use a decorators' brush to give it two generous layers of background colour, allowing each coat 2–4 hours to dry.

2 Trace the heart on p. 216, enlarge it on a photocopier and trace it off onto the surface.

3 To melt the wax, place a tablespoon in a jar in a pan of freshly boiled water. As it cools, you may have to replenish the water or keep it hot on an electric plate warmer. Never heat the wax over direct heat as it is highly inflammable.

4 Use an artists' fitch to paint the wax into the design. It will harden almost immediately. Do not use your favourite brush as it will probably be useless for painting afterwards.

5 Mix the topcoat and brush it on. Leave an hour or so to become touch-dry, then use a spatula to remove the wax, leaving the motif in the background colour.

6 To give an aged effect around the heart, rub back the topcoat slightly with wet and dry paper dipped in water.

❶ LEMON UNDER SAGE
The background is a mixture of 5tbsp white emulsion with 8tsp hansa yellow light, and the topcoat is 4tbsp white emulsion mixed with 1tbsp neutral grey and 1¼tsp phthalocyanine green. The resist is 1tbsp soft wax.

❷ CERULEAN UNDER AUBERGINE
This background is a mixture of 6tbsp white emulsion with 2tbsp phthalocyanine blue, and the topcoat is 2tbsp neutral grey, 4tsp raw umber and 2tsp dioxazine purple. The resist is the same as for swatch 1.

❶

❷

RESISTS

SPRAY-WAX RESIST

Using aerosol beeswax polish in conjunction with a stencil is easier for decorating large areas than using a painted-wax resist.

INGREDIENTS

See swatch captions. Colourants: artists' acrylic colours.

EQUIPMENT

Paint roller plus tray / stencil card / pencil / scalpel / cutting mat / tape measure / water-soluble crayon / repositionable spray adhesive / paper / beeswax aerosol polish / absorbent kitchen paper / container / 2 x 75mm (3in) decorators' brushes / rags / white spirit

INSTRUCTIONS

1 Prepare the surface thoroughly (see pp. 24–7) and use a roller to give it two coats of background colour.

2 Cut the simple motif below from stencil card and measure and mark out its positions on the wall.

3 Attach the stencil to the wall with spray adhesive, then protect the surroundings with paper. Spray the wax evenly into the stencil. Remove the stencil and blot excess wax from it using kitchen paper. To prevent wax from getting on the back of the stencil while you do this, lay it flat on a smooth surface such as a Formica-topped table or sheet of glass.

4 Carefully replace the stencil in the next-but-one position, spray with wax as before, then repeat for all alternate positions. Allow the wax 2–3 hours to harden off, then, if some is still wet, blot it up by pressing gently, not rubbing, with kitchen paper. Stencil the remaining sections.

5 Mix the paint and water colourwash, paint it over the wax resist (see pp. 124–5) and allow to dry (15–20 minutes).

6 Soak a rag in white spirit and rub the design very firmly to break through the paint and dissolve the wax below, leaving a slightly tinted broken-edged design.

❶ BRONZE
The background is 1 litre white emulsion and the topcoat is 270ml ready-mixed emulsion – BS 06 D 43 – diluted in the ratio 4 parts water : 1 part colour.

❷ DUSKY BLUE
Here the background is 1 litre white emulsion and the topcoat is 250ml white emulsion mixed with 2tsp black and 2tsp phthalocyanine blue, diluted as for swatch 1.

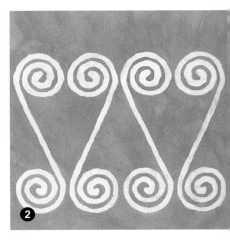

WHITING RESIST

A resist made from whiting, water and a pinch of wallpaper adhesive is a cheap and solvent-free alternative to wax, although it does not give quite such a refined finish. It makes a water-soluble paint which can be washed off very easily and leaves no residue. This means that you can wipe it off at any time during the procedure and also paint on further layers of paint or glazes, since no waxy residue will have been left.

INGREDIENTS | **See swatch captions. Colourants: artists' acrylic colours.**

EQUIPMENT | **Paint roller plus tray / paper / 1 small and 1 medium artists' brushes / pencil / tracing paper / screw-top jar / container / 1 x 100mm (4in) decorators' brush / spatula**

INSTRUCTIONS

1 Prepare the surface thoroughly (see pp. 24–7) and use a roller to give it two coats of background colour.

2 Use one of the artists' brushes to paint a flick of a freehand oval on paper, enlarge it on a photocopier and trace it meticulously onto the wall.

3 Combine all the resist ingredients in the jar, put the lid on securely, shake hard for 30 seconds, then leave to stand for 5 minutes. The resist should be thick and creamy. If it is too thin, add a little whiting; if too thick, more water.

4 Using the two artists' brushes, fill the motif with a copious layer of resist following the outline as accurately as you can. Leave to dry for an hour or more.

5 Mix up the topcoat and use a soft decorators' brush to paint on two coats. The resist will crumble easily, so do not be too robust. Allow each coat to dry (2–4 hours).

6 With a spatula, gently scrape away the resist and its covering of paint. It will come off in a powder which can be swept away and any residue washed off.

❶ **SALMON**
The background is 1 litre white emulsion, with a topcoat of 300ml white emulsion mixed with 150ml raw sienna and 5tsp magenta. The resist is 10tbsp whiting, 5tbsp water and 1tsp wallpaper paste.

❷ **BARLEY**
Here the background is again 1 litre white emulsion, with a topcoat of 400ml white emulsion mixed with 100ml yellow ochre. The resist is as in swatch 1.

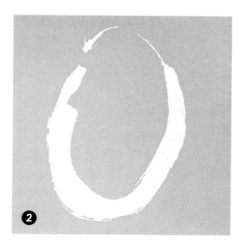

DECORATIVE AGEING

Ageing is a popular decorative finish, most commonly on wooden surfaces such as cupboard fronts, panelling or tables, but also on walls and floors. It works particularly well in an older home, where well-applied fresh paint can look out of place. These, then, are techniques to use for a finish that appears to have been around for a while.

When paint ages, its surface starts to wear away or bits drop off. In addition, the paint begins to acquire a patina and shine in places where it is frequently handled. For your ageing to appear authentic, follow examples of genuinely aged paintwork. The following techniques show how you can achieve a similar look.

RUBBING BACK

You can use wirewool, with or without wax, for a gently aged look on paintwork. As you rub, you break through the paint to reveal the surface below. If you use the wirewool with wax, be certain that you do not plan to apply further coats of paint, as few paints will adhere to wax.

Another method of ageing paint is to rub it with waterproof abrasive paper, usually referred to as wet and dry paper. Faster than using wirewool, this is probably the most subtle of our ageing techniques. It leaves the paint surface looking gently aged as well as wonderfully smooth. Only use the finest grades of paper and plenty of water.

The following recipes are for a panel approximately 4m² (43ft²).

See Part Two, p. 79, for rubbing off for a soft, all-over worn effect and p. 87 for rubbing back with cloth on 'set' paint.

INGREDIENTS

See swatch captions. Colourants: artists' acrylic colours.

EQUIPMENT

3 containers / 2 x 100mm (4in) decorators' brushes / tape measure / straightedge / water-soluble crayon or chalk line / 1 x 50mm (2in) decorators' brush / fine-grade wet and dry paper / large bowl of water / household sponge

INSTRUCTIONS

1 Prepare the surface thoroughly. See pp. 24–7.

2 Mix up each colour as you need it in a container.

3 Use the larger brushes to apply two coats each of the base and top colour, allowing each coat to dry (2–4 hours).

4 Decide on the position and dimensions of your stripe. Ours is 200mm (8in) wide, and 200mm (8in) from the top of the panel. Measure and mark it out using the tape measure, straightedge and the crayon (see p. 35).

5 Use the smaller decorators' brush to paint the stripe. Allow to dry overnight.

6 Dip a postcard-sized piece of wet and dry paper in water and use it to begin to rub away at the panelling. As you

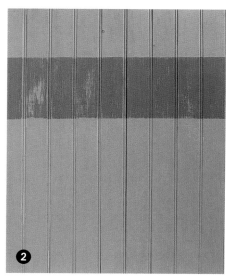

❶ OCHRE ON BUTTERMILK OVER BLACK Here, the base coat is 500ml black emulsion, with a topcoat of 300ml white emulsion, 200ml yellow ochre and 10tsp cadmium yellow. The stripe is 120ml yellow ochre.

❷ GREY ON GREY GREEN OVER DUSKY PINK This base coat is 450ml white emulsion and 4tsp each mars red and neutral grey. The top-coat is 350ml white emulsion and 120ml neutral grey. The stripe is 120ml neutral grey.

work, the paint will come off in a slurry and the piece of wet and dry paper will start to get clogged up. Mop the slurry up with the sponge, rinse the paper out, and continue with the rubbing until you are happy with the effect. The paint will rub off more quickly on corners and edges.

MELTED-WAX RESIST

This technique exploits the incompatibility of wax and water-based paint. The following recipes are for a panel approximately 4m² (43ft²). (See also pp. 84 and 90 in Part Two, where furniture polish is used for this effect and where wax under the base coat can reveal bare wood.)

INGREDIENTS **See swatch captions. Colourants: artists' acrylic colours.**

EQUIPMENT **3 containers / 2 x 100mm (4in) decorators' brushes / small glass jar / old saucepan / plate warmer (optional) / old artists' fitch / tape measure / straight-edge / water-soluble crayon or chalk line / 1 x 50mm (2in) decorators' brush / spatula / fine-grade wet and dry paper or fine wirewool / 2 tbsp beeswax**

INSTRUCTIONS

1 Prepare the surface thoroughly. See pp. 24–7.

2 Mix up each colour as you need it in a container.

3 Using one of the larger decorators' brushes, apply two coats of the base colour. Allow each coat to dry (2–4 hours).

4 Put the wax in the jar and the jar in a saucepan of boiling water. The wax will melt with the heat from the water. If necessary, keep the water hot by using a plate warmer. Alternatively, replace the water from time to time with freshly boiled water. Do not attempt to melt the wax over a

DECORATIVE AGEING

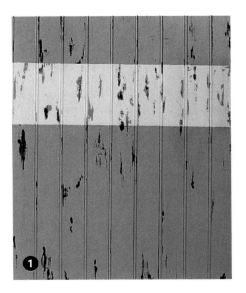

❷ PEACH ON STEEL OVER FLAME
Here the base coat is simply 500ml ready-mixed matt emulsion – BS 04 E 53 – and the top-coat is 500ml of another ready-mixed emulsion – BS 20 C 37. The stripe uses 120ml white emulsion combined with 1tsp each mars red and neutral grey. The resist is as for swatch 1.

❶ EAU DE NIL ON JADE OVER GREEN
This base coat uses 500ml ready-mixed matt emulsion – BS 14 C 53 – with a topcoat of 400ml white emulsion, 120ml raw umber, 2tsp phthalocyanine blue and 4tsp payne's grey. The stripe is 150ml white emulsion mixed with 2tsp cobalt blue and 1tsp yellow ochre. The resist is 3–6tbsp beeswax.

flame as there is a danger that it will catch light.

5 Using the artists' fitch, apply the melted wax loosely but thickly to the panelling in random shapes. These will become the areas where the paint will appear to have peeled off.

6 Once the wax is hard, use a large brush to apply two coats of the top colour, allowing 2–4 hours for each coat to dry.

7 Measure and mark out the 200mm (8in) wide stripe.

8 Apply further blobs of wax within the stripe, mostly over and around the wax which is already there.

9 Once the wax has hardened off, use the smaller decorators' brush to paint the stripe. Allow to dry (1 hour).

10 Next, use the spatula to scrape off the wax. You will easily be able to locate its thick layers beneath the paint. Of course, as you remove the wax, you will also take the paint with it, and this is what gives the piece its aged effect.

11 You can now use either a piece of wet and dry paper or wirewool dipped in beeswax to gently rub the whole paint surface back a little, smoothing off the sharp, new edges of paint left by the removal of the wax.

WHITING RESIST

Whiting mixed with water is a type of paint without a binder. When dry it can easily be scraped off with a spatula and it is water-soluble. Like wax it can be used as a resist for an aged effect. It does not produce such refined results, but it does have other advantages. One is that you can wipe it off easily at any stage, so if you do not like what you have done, you can remove it simply and cleanly. Secondly, because the whiting is water-based, it does not leave an oily or waxy residue. This means you can continue adding further coats of paint or glazes (see pp. 163–5). The following recipes cover approximately 4m² (43ft²).

INGREDIENTS See swatch captions. Colourants: artists' acrylic colours.

EQUIPMENT 3 containers / screw-top jar / 2 x 100mm (4in) decorators' brushes / artists' fitch / tape measure / straightedge / water-soluble crayon / 1 x 50mm (2in) decorators' brush / spatula / sponge / fine-grade wet and dry paper or fine wirewool / 2tbsp beeswax

INSTRUCTIONS **1–3** Follow the instructions for wax resist.

4 To make the resist, put the whiting, water and wallpaper paste in the screw-top jar. Put the lid on and shake vigorously for 30 seconds, then let the mixture stand for 5 minutes. If you find the mixture too thick or too thin – it should be thick and creamy – you can adjust the consistency by adding either water or whiting as appropriate.

5 Using the fitch, apply the resist in random blobs and shapes on top of the base colour. As with the wax resist, these areas will become those where the paint will appear to have peeled off. Leave to dry 1–2 hours.

6 Next, use another of the larger decorators' brushes to apply two coats of the top colour, allowing 2–4 hours for each coat to dry.

7 Measure and mark out the 200mm (8in) wide stripe.

8 Use the fitch to apply further blobs of resist to the stripe, mostly over and around the resist which is already there.

9 Once the resist has hardened off – about 1–2 hours – use the smaller decorators' brush to paint the stripe in the stripe colour. Allow to dry (1 hour).

10 Now use the spatula to carefully scrape off the resist and the paint layers with it. When you have finished, you will see that a residue of whiting is left on the surface. Wash this off with a wet sponge.

11 Finish as for the wax resist.

❶ SLATE ON BLUE OVER LILAC This base coat consists of 450ml white emulsion mixed with 1tbsp neutral grey and 1tsp dioxazine purple. The resist is 10tbsp whiting, 5tbsp water and 1tsp wallpaper paste. The topcoat is 500ml ready-mixed emulsion – BS 20 E 51 – while the stripes are 5tbsp payne's grey, 1tbsp white, 2tsp burnt umber and 1tbsp phthalocyanine green.

❷ SALMON ON EAU DE NIL OVER GREEN Here, the green base coat is also 500ml ready-mixed emulsion – BS 16 C 33 – and the topcoat is 450ml white emulsion mixed with 2tbsp cobalt blue and 1tbsp yellow ochre. The resist is as for swatch 1. The stripes are 150ml white emulsion mixed with 2tbsp naphthol red and 4tsp cadmium yellow.

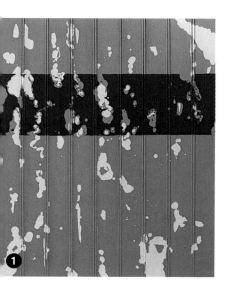

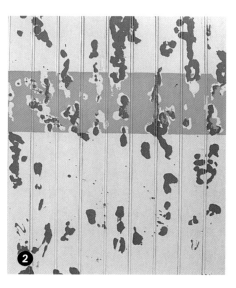

STENCILLED DESIGNS

Stencils are common decorators' devices. They are partly a way of controlling where your paint goes and partly a way of making repeat patterns. In these examples we have endeavoured to keep our stencils simple. This makes them easy to cut and also gives them a more modern look which we prefer.

When stencilling, use repositionable spray adhesive, both to hold the stencil in place as you work, and to stop paint seeping under its edges. Spray the back of the stencil lightly, protecting the surrounding surfaces with newspaper. The spray is highly toxic, so always spray in a well-ventilated area and avoid breathing it.

The following recipes are for approximately 500ml background colour and 7–8tbsp stencil colour – enough, probably, for an average wall. We have applied all our backgrounds with a roller.

INGREDIENTS

See swatch captions. Colourants: artists' acrylic colours.

EQUIPMENT

Choose from the following:
Large container / large paint roller plus tray / tracing paper / pencil / paper / stencil card / repositionable spray adhesive / cutting mat / scalpel / scissors / tape measure / ruler / pair of compasses / spirit level / water-soluble crayon / string / offcuts of card / masking tape / screw-top jars / saucers / sponges

SIMPLE STENCILLING

Perhaps the most commonly used design for a simple stencil is the *fleur-de-lis*, a favourite motif of interior designers and now a classic. Lettering has an equally long history as a decorative motif but also allows you an element of personalization. You could stencil your initials across a wall, floor, window or any other surface. The stencil is easy to cut and use, but a disciplined layout is essential for a classy look.

INSTRUCTIONS

1 Prepare the surface thoroughly. See pp. 24–7.
2 Trace the motifs from an alphabet in a lettering book or from an old manuscript. Plan the layout and the size of your stencil in unison. Our motif is 180 x 100mm (7 x 4in), cut from a piece of card 300 x 200mm (12 x 8in). To assist in top-to-bottom positioning, rule light lines 80mm (3¼in) below the required positions of the letters using a spirit level and water-soluble crayon (use string on large areas). Then cut the stencil motif with its lowest part 80mm (3¼in) up from the lower edge of the card. By placing this edge of the card on your marked line each time you stencil, you will always be assured of a correct position.
3 Spray the back of the stencil with adhesive and, starting

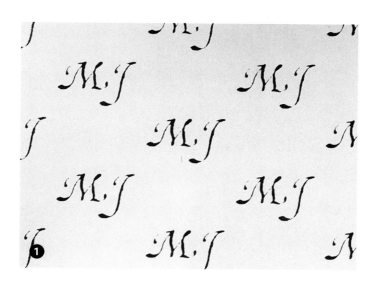

❶ GREY BLUE BACKGROUND AND DEEP MAGENTA For this background, mix 10tsp cobalt and 10tsp payne's grey into 500ml white emulsion. For the stencil colour – a surprisingly intense contrast against the background – add 4tsp white and 2tsp yellow ochre to 100ml magenta.

from the left, place it in its first position on one of the lines. Sponge in the colour and remove the stencil.

4 Use a spacing bar to determine side-to-side placements. This is an offcut of card attached to the side of the stencil with masking tape. Attach the spacing bar to the left of the stencil. Reposition your stencil to the right for the second print, aligning the left-hand end of the bar with the right-hand edge of the first motif. If you want a 250mm (10in) space between motifs, then the left-hand end of the bar should be 250mm (10in) from the left edge of the cut-out motif in the stencil card. Sponge in as before.

To stencil to the left of your first image, you will have to attach the spacing bar to the right-hand side of the stencil.

5 Repeat along the marked lines until you have completed your design. Note how, in our example, each stencilled image is set half a space along from the one above.

OVERLAPPING STENCILS

Simple stencils can be designed to link up to create flowing borders. Here, a tendril and a flower have been stencilled together along a line.

INSTRUCTIONS

1 Prepare the surface thoroughly. See pp. 24–7.

2 Trace each motif on page 216 separately, together with their registration holes. Enlarge them on a photocopier and use to make the stencils (see p. 36). The registration holes should be carefully positioned on each stencil.

3 Rule a line along the wall at the height you would like your border and place one of the stencils on it with its holes over the line. Lightly mark the wall through the registration holes, using a water-soluble crayon.

❶ PALE YELLOW BACKGROUND WITH FUCHSIA PINK
The background is 1tbsp each hansa yellow light and raw umber with 550ml white emulsion. The tendrils are in 4tbsp white, 2tbsp raw umber, 1½tbsp payne's grey and 1tbsp phthalocyanine green. The flower is 100ml magenta with 4tsp white and 2tsp yellow ochre.

❷ LABURNUM BACKGROUND WITH BLUE GREY
The background is 500ml BS 10 E 50 emulsion with tendrils in 100ml magenta with 5tsp burnt sienna. The flowers are 6tbsp white and 1tbsp payne's grey.

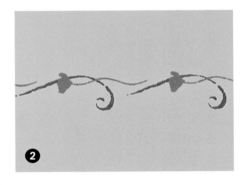

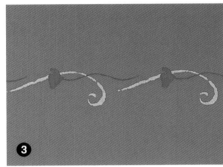

4 Move the stencil along the line towards the right until the right-hand mark shows through the left-hand hole. Mark the wall again through the right-hand hole. Continue in this fashion until you have set all the registration marks along the ruled line.

5 Beginning with the tendril, lightly spray the back of the stencil and place it in its first position, lining it up so that its holes are over the first two marks. Sponge in the colour.

6 Move the tendril stencil to the next-but-one position, and sponge this in the same way, and so on along the line. By the time you reach the end, the first stencilled tendrils will have dried sufficiently for you to stencil those in between.

7 The flower stencil is sponged in over the top of the tendril, using exactly the same registration marks.

❸ BRONZE BACKGROUND WITH BLUE
The base coat is 500ml BS 06 D 43 emulsion with tendrils in 6tbsp white, 2tbsp hansa yellow light and ¼tsp raw umber. The flowers are 4tbsp white, 4tbsp cobalt blue and 1tsp dioxazine purple.

SHADED STENCILLING

A second colour sponged over the first can give a simple, flat stencil a three-dimensional look. These shaded circles and squares have soft edges as their stencils have been torn into shape rather than cut.

INSTRUCTIONS

1 Prepare the surface thoroughly. See pp. 24–7.

2 To make the stencils, draw a 50mm (2in) diameter circle and a 100mm (4in) square on separate pieces of stencil card. Begin by making a hole in the centre of each card, then delicately tear out the shapes as close as possible to the line.

3 Tear two strips of card, each about 150 x 40mm (6 x 1½in), down their long edge.

4 Plan the spacing of your motifs and use a washable crayon to mark out the surface to be decorated. The squares here are spaced at 100mm (4in) intervals and the circles at 50mm (2in). When positioning the motifs, use the spacing bar method (see p. 157).

5 To stencil a circle, attach the circle stencil with spray adhesive and sponge quite densely using the first colour. With the stencil still in place, take a sponge sparsely loaded with the second colour and dab it in, starting on one side of the circle and gradually moving inwards. Aim to create a gentle gradation of tone which follows the form of the circle, transforming it into a ball.

6 For a square, place the stencil in position and lightly sponge in the first colour. With the stencil still in place, position one of the strips of card across the diagonal, leaving the lower, triangular half of the square exposed. Sponge this in densely with the same colour.

7 Reposition the strip across the other diagonal, leaving the opposite lower half exposed, and sponge this in lightly with the second colour.

8 Place the second strip across the first, leaving a small triangle exposed on the bottom edge of the square. Sponge this in densely with the second colour. Remove all the strips of card to reveal a pyramid with each face in a different colour made up of the various layers and densities of paint.

❶ SUGARED ALMOND BACKGROUND
The background is BS 04 B 15 emulsion and the first stencil colour is 4tbsp white, 2tbsp cobalt and 1tbsp yellow ochre. The second requires 5tbsp hansa yellow light, 2tbsp white, 2tsp yellow ochre and ½tsp raw umber.

❷ SHELL PINK BACKGROUND
This background is BS 04 B 17 emulsion and the first colour is 6tbsp white, 1tbsp ultra-marine, 2tbsp dioxazine purple, and 1½tsp black. The second colour is 4tbsp white, 4tbsp mars red and 1tbsp cadmium yellow medium.

❸ HEATHER GREY BACKGROUND
The background is BS 04 B 21 emulsion and the blue is 6tbsp ultramarine, 3tbsp white and 1½tsp quin-acridone violet. The acid yellow uses a mixture of 4tbsp white, 4tsp hansa yellow light and ¼tsp raw umber.

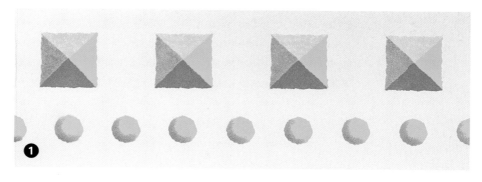

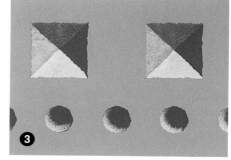

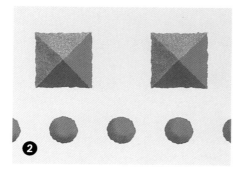

SEASIDE DOORS DESIGN

Even if you live far from the coast, this treatment for doors will give you an appetite for long summer days on the beach. More Mediterranean than British, more California than New England, the colours have been chosen to bring a sunny atmosphere into any interior. If you are anxious to create the look of real weatherbeaten beach-hut doors, you will need thick base coats of emulsion to give you plenty of leeway when you are rubbing back. Over these we have stencilled a distant view of a boat in full sail, and a close-up of its stripy flag. Keep the painting loose. It should look as if it had to be painted quickly. Holidays are not for work.

BASIC RECIPE – SAND ON SKY BLUE

PREPARATION

Prepare the surface thoroughly. See pp. 24–7.

INGREDIENTS

For 2 standard cupboard doors
**First base coat ▶ 300ml white vinyl matt emulsion / 3tbsp ultramarine artists' acrylic colour
Second base coat ▶ 300ml white vinyl matt emulsion / 3tbsp yellow ochre artists' acrylic colour
Sails, hull and flag (colours not mixed together) ▶ 1tbsp white artists' acrylic colour / 1tbsp ultramarine artists' acrylic colour / scant ¼tsp naphthol red artists' acrylic colour**

EQUIPMENT

2 large screw-top jars / 2 x 75mm (3in) decorators' brushes / fine-grade wet and dry paper / 1 household sponge and 3 smaller pieces / rag / tracing paper / pencil / paper / repositionable spray adhesive / stencil card / scalpel / cutting mat / ruler / water-soluble crayon / 3 saucers / small artists' brush / masking tape

INSTRUCTIONS
Base coats

1 As you will be applying thick coats of paint which are liable to run, remove your cupboard doors and work on them on a horizontal surface.
2 Mix up each of the base-coat colours in the screw-top jars. You should have sufficient to apply two good thick coats of each colour.
3 Fully load one of the decorators' brushes with paint and apply a generous layer of the first colour. Do not worry about brush marks, but in fact aim to leave them showing. However, be organized in the order in which you paint. Start with the door panels, followed by the cross rails, then the stiles. Finally, paint the edges. Always finish by brushing out

the paint in the same direction as the grain of the wood. Leave to dry. Emulsion paint can normally be re-coated after 4 hours but you may need to leave the thicker coats used here for a little longer.

4 The doors will need a second coat of blue, applied in the same way, followed by two coats of yellow. After the final coat, leave to harden off for a day.

5 To create the weatherbeaten look of a beach hut, rub the final yellow coat with the wet and dry paper dipped in water (see pp. 152–3). This not only leaves a flat, matt finish, but also breaks through the yellow to reveal the blue brush marks below. You can rub off extra yellow in those places where paint would have worn more quickly – for example, around handles and along edges. As you do this, a slurry of paint and water will form which you should wipe off with a wet sponge as you proceed.

6 Once you are satisfied with the look of the doors, dry them off with a rag.

Boat motif

1 Trace the designs for the boat and the flag (see p. 217), enlarge them on a photocopier and use them to make the stencils (see p. 36).

2 Using the ruler and the water-soluble crayon, measure and mark the position of the boat in the centre of the door panel. Position the boat stencil 30mm (1¼in) below and to the right of it as required for the shadow, then sponge the shadow in lightly, using 1tbsp of the base coat yellow mixed on a saucer with a tiny amount of yellow ochre, just enough to take it down a tone.

3 The shadow will dry quickly, so within a few minutes you can reposition the stencil to paint in the boat itself. Sponge in the hull using the ultramarine blue spooned onto a saucer.

4 Sponge the sails in white in the same way, then use the small artists' brush to flick on their red stripes.

Flag motif

1 For the striped flag, apply masking tape to leave a central rectangle. Its size will be governed by the size of your door panel. Sponge the rectangle in white.

2 Position the flag stencil – the wavy lines – on top of the white sponged rectangle, and sponge it in using the ultramarine. Remove the stencil and the masking tape and allow to dry (1 hour).

3 For the shadow, apply masking tape inside the bottom and right-hand edges of the flag, with another line of tape about 30mm (1¼in) from the first, to create an L-shaped

❶ SAND ON SKY BLUE
The basic recipe.

❷ SKY BLUE ON SAND
If you prefer sky blues to golden sands, simply reverse the base and top coats. Everything else remains the same, except of course for the shadows which you make by adding a smidgen of ultramarine to a tablespoon of the blue topcoat.

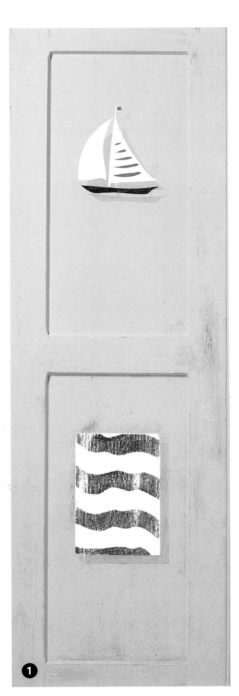

area. Sponge this in, using the same yellow as you used for the boat's shadow. Both this shadow and that of the boat should give the impression of the boat and flag floating in front of the door on a sunny day.

4 If the boat and flag look a little too freshly painted, you can use the wet and dry paper again with water to give them a worn and weatherbeaten look. But gently does it – the layers of paint here are much thinner than the paint of the base coats, and if you are too vigorous, you will remove the boat and flag completely.

FOSSIL TABLE DESIGN

This design idea takes the stone-finish technique of pp. 94–5 a step further, by setting an authentic-looking fossil ammonite into a stone-finished table top. Fossils are most commonly found in limestones. The limestones vary so much in colour and texture that there is bound to be one that you like. We mimic one that leans towards pink, and another that leans towards yellow. The third is more granite than limestone, but you can be more fanciful with your colouring if you wish.

Fossils are beautiful but delicate and fragile. The use of thick paint over a whiting resist can readily create an effect which mimics their appearance. Be confident in the handling of your brush and in the application of the paint, and do not worry about drips or splashes, or misplaced resist. Anything can have happened to the fossil during the last 250 million years. And if you want to make your fossil bigger, then go ahead. They could grow to over 2m (6½ft) across.

BASIC RECIPE – PINK-TINTED LIMESTONE

PREPARATION **Prepare the surface thoroughly. See pp. 24–7.**

INGREDIENTS *For a small table*
Base coat ▶ 6tbsp white vinyl matt emulsion / 1tsp raw sienna artists' acrylic colour
Resist ▶ 10tsp whiting / 5tsp water / ½tsp wallpaper paste
First colour ▶ 6tbsp white vinyl matt emulsion / 5tsp raw sienna artists' acrylic colour / methylated spirits
Second colour ▶ 6tbsp white vinyl matt emulsion / 2tsp raw sienna artists' acrylic colour / 2tsp raw umber artists' acrylic colour / methylated spirits
Dabs ▶ scant ¼tsp each mars red, yellow ochre and raw umber artists' acrylic colours
Protective coat ▶ 1tbsp wax polish

EQUIPMENT **3 containers / coarse-textured paint roller plus tray / tracing paper / paper / hard pencil / chalk / screw-top jar / 1 x 6mm (¼in) round artists' brush / stencil card / repositionable spray adhesive / scalpel / cutting mat / 1 x 25mm (1in) old, stiff decorators' brush / spatula / 3 household sponges and 6 smaller pieces / bowl of water / plant mister / fine-grade wet and dry paper / soft cloth**

INSTRUCTIONS **1** Mix up the base colour in one of the containers. Use the
Base coats roller to apply two coats to the table top and its edges, allowing 2–4 hours for each coat to dry.
2 Trace the ammonite design from p. 217, enlarge it on a photocopier to fit your table, then trace it onto the table top, using tracing paper, a hard pencil and chalk.

① PINK-TINTED LIMESTONE
The basic recipe gives a pinkish limestone. We have been quite free with the addition of the dabs of colour, especially the mars red. The position of the ammonite on the table top is, of course, a matter of personal preference. Here, we have placed it in one corner.

② YELLOW-TINTED LIMESTONE
Here we positioned the ammonite in the middle of the table and used a base coat of 6tbsp white emulsion mixed with ½tsp yellow ochre and ½tsp raw umber, a first colour of 6tbsp white emulsion with 1tsp raw umber and 2tsp yellow ochre, and dabs of yellow ochre, white and mid-grey. The second colour was made from 6tbsp white emulsion with 2tsp neutral grey and ½tsp yellow ochre, and coloured dabs as before.

③ GREY-TINTED LIMESTONE
This swatch is based on swatch 2 on p. 94 but uses stronger colours and a more vigorous method to create this textured, decorative finish. The base coat is made of 6tbsp white emulsion with 2tsp neutral grey. The first colour is 2tbsp white emulsion with 4tbsp payne's grey and 4tsp burnt umber. The second colour consists of 1tbsp white artists' acrylic colour, dabbed and spread to create a misty effect.

Resist
Mix the whiting, water and wallpaper paste in a screw-top jar to make the resist (see pp. 151). Use the round artists' brush to loosely paint the resist onto the sections left white on the design you have copied. Apply it quite thickly and do not worry about being neat. Leave to dry for a few hours.

Stencil

1 Meanwhile, use your traced design to make a stencil of the ammonite outline (see p. 36). Position the stencil on the table top over the ammonite, holding it in place with spray adhesive.

2 Using the old decorators' brush, apply a thick layer of the base coat into the stencil and over the resist. In order to mimic the texture and pattern of the ammonite, brush the paint out so that it makes curved ridges running from the inner edge of the spiral to the outer edge. An old stiff brush is better for applying this layer than a new one as it leaves good brush marks. If the brush marks disappear, allow to dry for a few moments, then repeat the process. Remove the stencil with care.

3 Splatter a few flicks of the base coat across the table top at random if you want further texture. Allow to harden for at least 4 hours, though it may take longer than normal as the paint has been applied so thickly.

4 Use the spatula and a damp sponge gently to remove the dried whiting resist together with its covering of paint. This will reveal the ammonite, convincingly textured, but as yet without colour.

Stone finish

1 Mix up the emulsion and raw sienna in a container to make the first colour, and the emulsion, raw sienna and raw umber in another container to make the second colour. Complete the stone finish with these two colours, following the instructions on pp. 94–5 and 132. Apply each colour with a sponge across the whole of the table top, including the ammonite, as well as over the edges of the table. Sponge or splash with water, spray with methylated spirits and apply sponged-on dabs of mars red, yellow ochre and raw umber as required. Aim for an open texture with plenty of variation. Take care not be too heavy-handed. You should try to achieve a subtle effect.

2 The ammonite will by now be almost camouflaged. To reveal it, very carefully rub away some of the two colours from the ridges, using the wet and dry paper dipped in water. This will give a worn look. You can accentuate the three-dimensional qualities by rubbing away a little more from one side of the spiral than from the other. However, care is called for, as the coats are quite thin. You should also guard against rubbing away at other parts of the table top.

Protective coat

Leave aside for 24 hours, then buff up the whole of the table top with wax polish applied on a soft cloth.

ROSE DES VENTS

Rose des vents is the poetic expression the French use to describe a compass card. This motif traditionally decorates the uncarpeted floor of an entrance hall. We chose to paint our design on chipboard with a stone-effect finish for two reasons. The first is that the texture of chipboard lends itself well to the rough finish of stone. The second that chipboard is normally laid in panels, each of which can become a slab of stone. The result is a starring role for a functional but not attractive material normally used as a base for other floor surfaces.

BASIC RECIPE – VENETIAN RED, BLUE AND GREEN ON SANDSTONE

PREPARATION

Prepare the surface thoroughly. See pp. 24–7.

INGREDIENTS

To cover approximately 4–5m² (43–54ft²)
Base coat ▶ 500ml white vinyl matt emulsion / 5tsp raw sienna artists' acrylic colour
First colour ▶ 200ml white vinyl matt emulsion / 4tsp raw sienna artists' acrylic colour / methylated spirits
Second colour ▶ 200ml white vinyl matt emulsion / 4tsp raw sienna artists' acrylic colour / 10tsp raw umber artists' acrylic colour / methylated spirits
Dabs ▶ 1tsp raw umber artists' acrylic colour / 1tsp raw sienna artists' acrylic colour / 1tsp mars red artists' acrylic colour
Medium star ▶ 2tbsp phthalocyanine green artists' acrylic colour / 1tbsp black artists' acrylic colour / 2tsp yellow ochre artists' acrylic colour / 2tsp white artists' acrylic colour
Circle and small star ▶ 1tbsp magenta artists' acrylic colour / 1tbsp mars red artists' acrylic colour / 2tsp white artists' acrylic colour
Large star ▶ 1tbsp white artists' acrylic colour / 1tbsp cobalt blue artists' acrylic colour / ¼tsp dioxazine purple artists' acrylic colour
Protective coat ▶ 1 litre acrylic floor varnish

EQUIPMENT

3 large containers / coarse-textured paint roller plus tray / 2 household sponges plus 6 pieces / bowl of water / plant mister / plate / tracing paper / paper / chalk / hard pencil / 3 screw-top jar / 3 medium flat artists' brushes / 3 small round artists' brushes / fine-grade wet and dry paper / 1 x 100mm (4in) varnish brush

INSTRUCTIONS
Base coats

Mix the base colour in a large container and use the roller to apply two coats, allowing 4 hours for each coat to dry.

Stone finish

1 Mix the first colour in another large container. Following the instructions for stone finishes on pp. 94–5, apply it to the floor using a sponge, adding water, spraying on methylated spirits, and dabbing on the raw umber, raw sienna and mars

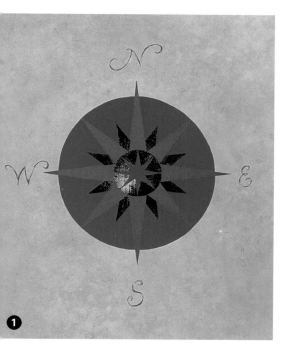

red from the plate. We have sponged the texture in quite evenly, but if you prefer a rugged look to your stone, be a bit freer with the sponge and water.

2 Mix the second colour in the third large container and apply it in the same way, again adding in the sponged dabs. Take care not to be too heavy-handed. You should aim for a subtle effect. Allow to dry (4 hours).

Motifs

1 Trace the compass design (see p. 217), and enlarge it as required on a photocopier. Trace the compass-point initials you require from a book of lettering. The outer circle in our example measures 320mm (12¾in) in diameter. Transfer the design to the floor using tracing paper, chalk and a hard pencil (see p. 35), ensuring that it is correctly orientated.

2 Mix up the stars and circle colours in the screw-top jars. Use the artists' brushes to paint in the centre and points of the medium star, then allow to dry (1 hour).

3 Using the wet and dry paper, rub the paint back lightly to reveal parts of the base colour as highlights.

4 Now you may well have lost some of your tracing. Retrace as necessary, then paint in the other parts of the design using the appropriate colours and brushes.

5 Finally, use a small round artists' brush to paint the initials of the compass points in the same colour as the circle.

Protective coat

Use the varnish brush and follow the manufacturers' instructions to apply a minimum of three coats of varnish.

❶ VENETIAN RED, BLUE AND GREEN ON SANDSTONE The basic recipe. Here, the small touch of ageing on the green star helps push the colour back, leaving the red and blue star looking as if they are floating above it. The colours are in keeping with the period look of the design and lettering.

❷ BLACK AND WHITE ON GREY LIMESTONE For the grey limestone effect, follow the recipe on p. 94. All you will need to colour the motif is 2tbsp black to paint in the large star, and 4tbsp white for the circle and the small star.

PAINTING ON GLASS

To judge by the tenacity with which splashes of paint cling to windows, one would imagine that you could decorate glass with almost any paint. But specialist glass paints – opaque for signwriting, transparent for stained-glass effects, and frosting varnish for an etched-glass look – are available. It is these last two that we have used for our designs.

You can apply the paint with either a brush or a sponge. It is very liquid, so any masking must be really well stuck down to prevent the paint seeping behind. Once the painting is complete, found objects such as leaves or postage stamps can be stuck between this sheet and a second one, the two held together with foldback clips.

The recipes will decorate a sheet of glass 300mm² (12in²).

PAINTED GLASS FRAMES

INGREDIENTS   **See swatch captions.**

EQUIPMENT   **Ruler / pencil / paper / 2 sheets of glass, 300 x 300mm (12 x 12in) / masking tape / saucer / small piece of household sponge, trimmed of its corners / small, round artists' brush / solvent for glass paint / 4 foldback clips with removable levers**

INSTRUCTIONS   1 Prepare the surface thoroughly. See pp. 24–7.
2 Draw a 300mm (12in) square on a sheet of paper and within this square rule a noughts and crosses grid of four lines at 100mm (4in) intervals. Rule a further four lines, 10mm (⅜in) out from the first.
3 Copy the motif on p. 217. Either trace it onto or glue photocopies of it in the centre of each of the corners of the grid you have drawn.
4 Attach the drawing to the back of one of the pieces of glass and hold it in place with tape at the centre of each edge. Place the glass face up on a level surface.
5 Tear masking tape along its length and stick it firmly on the glass along the first set of grid lines, leaving the four corners exposed.
6 Pour a little of the first colour onto a saucer and use a small piece of household sponge to apply it to each of the corners. You must paint it on in one go. Any attempts to apply a second coat will only result in the first coat being disturbed or removed. Leave to harden (1 hour), then remove the masking tape.
7 Using the artists' brush and the second colour, paint in lines of dots at approximately 10mm (⅜in) intervals along the second set of lines. Load the brush fully and just dab it onto the surface to make the dot. Allow to dry (2 hours). As soon

❶ GOLDEN OLIVE CORNERS
All the colours are ready-mixed glass paints bought in 50ml bottles. The first colour is olive green, the second violet and the third turquoise.

❷ SLATE GREY CORNERS
Again, the colours are ready-mixed glass paints. The first is grey, the second magenta and the third golden brown.

as you have completed the dots, clean the brush out with solvent, otherwise the paint will harden in the bristles and the brush will be of no further use.

8 With the artists' brush and the third colour, paint in each of the spirals. Again, fully load the brush and let the paint flow off it as you follow the line of the design seen through the glass. Allow to dry (2 hours). Immediately clean the brush with solvent as before.

9 You can now assemble the frame, but the paint will not be fully cured for a number of days, so you should be sure to handle the glass with care. As well as applying painted decoration, we have used the two pieces of glass to trap small decorative items – postage stamps and leaves in these examples. These have been stuck in place on the second piece of glass. Hold the two pieces together with the foldback clips, then remove their levers.

❸ BRONZE METALLIC CORNERS
Here the first colour is 50ml frosting varnish mixed with a scant ¼tsp bronze powder, and the second and third colours are both grey glass paint.

PART FOUR

PROJECTS

An inspiring array of ideas for decorating every surface in the home – walls, floors, doors, windows, furniture and accessories – each in a choice of colourways to show what can be achieved.

To paint this seedhead frieze (see pp. 180–3), we used a large stencil in a rather unusual way. Instead of stencilling on paint, as you might expect, we filled the stencil area with sprayed-on beeswax resist, then followed it with paint. For a smaller design you could apply ordinary wax with a spatula.

CHEQUERBOARD
WALL

Do not let anyone persuade you that papering a wall is quicker and easier than stamping a design on it. Even if it were true, papering will never match the pleasure to be had from making your own stamp and using it across a wall. The end result will always have a quality that cannot be matched by any wallpaper. It will never be as perfect as, nor will it have the complexity of a wallpaper pattern, but if that is what you like, the chances are that you are reading this book by accident.

This simple stamp needs few registration marks. Once you have drawn the horizontals and a vertical on your wall, you can proceed, only stopping to swap to the smaller stamps to negotiate awkward corners, fixtures and fittings.

BASIC RECIPE – STRAW ON OPAL

PREPARATION

Prepare the surface thoroughly. See pages 24–7.

INGREDIENTS

For a wall up to 4m² (43ft²)
Base coats ▸ 600ml white vinyl matt emulsion / 1tbsp cobalt blue artists' acrylic colour / 2tbsp yellow ochre artists' acrylic colour / 2tbsp payne's grey artists' acrylic colour
Motif ▸ 225ml white vinyl matt emulsion / 1tbsp hansa yellow light artists' acrylic colour / 1tbsp raw umber artists' acrylic colour
Optional protective coat ▸ 300ml matt acrylic varnish

EQUIPMENT

2 large containers / 1 large paint roller plus tray / 1 x 50mm (2in) decorators' brush / plumb line / spirit level / water-soluble crayon / 200 x 200mm (8 x 8in) foam-rubber mat / scissors or scalpel / cutting mat / foam-core or marine-ply backing board / small tube contact adhesive / small paint roller / newspaper / masking tape / 1 x 50mm (2in) varnish brush (optional)

CHEQUERBOARD WALL

INSTRUCTIONS

Base coats

1 Mix up the colour for the base coat in one of the containers and stir well.

2 Apply two even coats to the wall with the large roller. Use the decorators' brush to apply paint around any fixtures and into corners. Allow 4 hours for each coat to dry.

Design

1 Plan the layout of the pattern on the wall (see p. 35), using the plumb line to set a vertical guide and the spirit level and a water-soluble crayon to mark the horizontals.

2 Use the foam-rubber mat to make three stamps, one with four stripes 150 x 150mm (6 x 6in), one with one stripe 150 x 21mm (6 x ¾in), and one with half a stripe, 75 x 21mm (3 x ¾in). Attach them to backing boards of foam core or marine ply with contact adhesive (see p. 38).

3 Mix up the motif colour in the other container and stir well. Apply the paint to the square stamp using the small paint roller (see p. 39).

4 Following the vertical guide, stamp a line of motifs on your wall, re-applying paint to the stamp for each motif. Do not forget to turn the stamp through 90° for alternate motifs in order to create the chequerboard effect. Repeat until most of the wall is covered. The square stamp will cover large areas of wall, but as you come up against corners or fixtures such as light switches, you will need to use the smaller stamps to complete the design, perhaps in conjunction with newspaper to mask off areas that you have already completed.

Notes To prevent the paint drying on your stamps if you decide to take a break while you are working, you should first gently clean them by dabbing them up and down in a bowl of water, then pat them dry on kitchen paper.

If your wall is in a location where it is likely to be knocked, kicked or scuffed, use the varnish brush to give it a coat of varnish for protection.

1 STRAW ON OPAL
The basic recipe.

2 OPAL ON STRAW
Here the emphasis has been subtly shifted by reversing the basic colourway, printing the blue onto the yellow. Not only does the balance between the colours alter, making the blue more dominant, but the texture shifts to the blue as well.

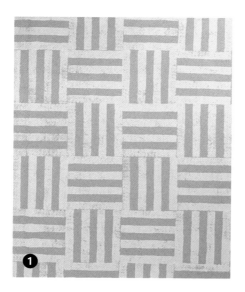

3 STONE ON BRICK RED
These are the more robust colours of building materials – stone and red bricks. The strong contrast will make a splash in any room, so may need to be confined to a small area, or used to animate a dead corner. The red consists of 300ml ready-mixed emulsion – BS 04 E 53– mixed with 5tbsp burnt sienna and 8tsp white. The stone colour is made from 300ml white emulsion coloured with 1tbsp raw umber.

4 WHITE ON STONE
This combination results in far less contrast. Pale colours such as these are more suited to large areas, while the subdued pattern will not clash with pictures on the wall. The base colour is the stone used in swatch 3, overprinted with white emulsion. Couldn't be much simpler than that.

WHIMSICAL WINDOW
SURROUND

The design for this window frame has four unequal sections, each one wrapped around the corner of the window opening. The overlapping shapes are created by masking with torn paper and masking tape. Where the overlaps occur, a darker area results which we have stencilled with a diamond motif. The outer edge of the design is masked entirely using torn paper, but where sections overlap, we masked one of the edges with masking tape to give a straight edge.

You can, of course, adapt a project like this to suit any size or shape of window and we recommend that, if you are decorating more than one window in a room, you should vary the masking from window to window to avoid a regimented appearance.

BASIC RECIPE – RASPBERRY, SALMON AND PEA GREEN

PREPARATION	**Prepare the surface thoroughly. See pages 24–7.**
INGREDIENTS	*For an average window and its surround* **Background ▶ 500ml ready-mixed pinkish-grey vinyl matt emulsion (BS 04 B 15)** **First colour ▶ 6tbsp white vinyl matt emulsion / 2tbsp cadmium yellow artists' acrylic colour / 1½tsp cobalt blue artists' acrylic colour / 1½tsp raw umber artists' acrylic colour / acrylic scumble and water (see instructions)** **Second colour ▶ 100ml white vinyl matt emulsion / 2tsp raw umber artists' acrylic colour / 2tsp mars red artists' acrylic colour / acrylic scumble and water (see instructions)** **Third colour ▶ 4tbsp white vinyl matt emulsion / 4tbsp magenta artists' acrylic colour / 2tsp raw umber artists' acrylic colour / 2tsp raw sienna artists' acrylic colour / acrylic scumble and water (see instructions)**
EQUIPMENT	**Masking tape / medium-textured paint roller plus tray / 1 x 50mm (2in) decorators' brush / paper / tape measure / repositionable spray adhesive / 3 screw-top jars / small, fine-textured paint roller plus tray / 3 x 25mm (1in) decorators' brushes / 3 large, deep plates / 6 x 75mm (3in) decorators' brushes**
INSTRUCTIONS **Background**	1 Mask off the window frame with masking tape. 2 Using the medium paint roller and the medium decorators' brush for the corners, paint the surrounding wall and the window opening with the background colour.
Masking	1 Begin at the bottom right-hand corner by masking with a

176

vertical strip of torn paper on the face of the wall, 100–150mm (4–6in) away from the window opening (see pp. 40–1). Attach with a light spray of adhesive. Run a horizontal line of masking tape across the face of the wall and into the window opening to finish this area of masking with a straight line.

2 Mask beneath the window with a band of torn paper running across the sill and down the face of the wall below the window. Take it down to the skirting if you wish.

3 Mask off the top left-hand section in a similar manner, again using a torn-paper mask, its lower edge finished with a straight, horizontal line of masking tape.

Painting

1 Mix the first colour in a screw-top jar, and use the small roller in conjunction with a 25mm (1in) decorators' brush to paint the bottom right-hand section. Apply two coats, allowing 2–4 hours for each coat to dry.

2 Dilute 1tbsp of the first colour with an equal amount of scumble plus 4tbsp water on a deep plate. Use a 75mm (3in) brush to colourwash the masked-off upper left-hand section, and brush off with a clean, soft 75mm (3in) brush and a 25mm (1in) brush for the corners (see pp. 124–5). Apply a second coat of colourwash, allowing 2 hours between coats. Remove all the masking from the wall and opening, but leave it in place at the very top left-hand corner as further coats of

❶ LILAC, SIENNA AND CREAM OVER GARNET
The background is 500ml ready-mixed garnet emulsion – BS 04 D 44. The first colour is 5tbsp white emulsion, plus 1¼tsp raw umber and 2½tsp each raw and burnt sienna. The second colour is 120ml white emulsion, with ½tsp each dioxazine purple and payne's grey, while the third colour is 120ml white emulsion with 2tsp raw umber.

paint are to be applied here. Allow the second coat of colourwash to dry (4 hours).

3 Mask off the two remaining sections in a similar fashion, allowing the new masking to overlap the adjoining sections.

4 Mix the second and third colours in screw-top jars. Dilute a few tablespoons of each colour with equal parts of scumble and 4 parts water on plates. Using the same technique as in step 2, give two coats of colourwash to the top right-hand section with the diluted second colour, and two to the bottom left-hand section with the diluted third colour.

5 The top corners of the window are painted in the undiluted version of their colourwash. The torn-paper masks that are still in place will create their soft edges. For their straight edges, use masking tape placed horizontally and vertically in line with the window opening. Use a small decorators' brush to paint each corner. Remove all masking.

6 At each place where the colours overlap at the sides and at the top, use four pieces of torn paper to mask off a loose diamond motif. Attach the pieces of torn paper to the wall with spray adhesive and paint each of the diamonds in one of the three colours using a small decorators' brush.

❷ GREY, CAFÉ AU LAIT AND AQUA OVER OFF-WHITE
This background is 500ml white emulsion lightly tinted with 4tsp neutral grey. The first colour is 120ml white emulsion with 1tsp ultramarine and ½tsp yellow ochre. The second colour is 120ml white emulsion mixed with 2tsp each burnt sienna and payne's grey, and the third colour is 6tbsp white emulsion, plus 2tbsp ultramarine and 1tbsp yellow ochre.

Window frame

Remove the masking from the window frame and use one of the 25mm (1in) decorators' brushes to give it two coats of the second colour, allowing 2–4 hours for each coat to dry.

LATE-SUMMER
SEEDHEAD FRIEZE

For many of us, this design is reminiscent of the autumn nature collections we made as children and displayed in jars in the school art room. There may be fewer wild flowers about now, but the memory of them can become a permanent installation thanks to this delicate hedgerow of painted seedheads.

BASIC RECIPE – GOLDEN HAY

PREPARATION

Prepare the surface thoroughly. (See pp. 24–7.) Apply two coats of paint to the wall in a colour that will complement the frieze.

INGREDIENTS

To cover approximately 4m² (43ft²)
Base coat ▶ 500ml thick, white, non-drip vinyl matt emulsion
Resist ▶ aerosol can of beeswax
Colourwash and shadows ▶ 10tsp hansa yellow light artists' acrylic colour / 1tsp raw umber artists' acrylic colour
Protective coat ▶ 250ml clear polish or beeswax

EQUIPMENT

Paper / tape measure / repositionable spray adhesive / 2 x 100mm (4in) decorators' brushes / plasterers' float or trowel / tracing paper / pencil / paper / scalpel / stencil card / cutting mat / water-soluble crayon / absorbent kitchen paper / screw-top jar / large container / saucer / household sponge / soft rags / white spirit / lint-free cloth

INSTRUCTIONS
Base coat

1 Use torn paper to mask off the area above the frieze. This will create a soft, natural edge in keeping with the design. Do not be tempted to use old newspaper, as the spray adhesive may dissolve the ink and transfer yesterday's news onto your clean wall. Instead, use lining paper or the clean side of old photocopies. Set the torn edge of the paper about 600mm (24in) up from the skirting board and attach it with the spray adhesive.
2 Use a decorators' brush to apply a thick layer of the emulsion to the wall beneath the paper and spread it out using the plasterers' float. The aim is to create a patchy texture with vertical marks running up and down the design. Leave to dry overnight.

Stencil

1 Trace the seedhead design (see p. 218), enlarge it on a photocopier and make it into a stencil (see p. 36). Do not forget to cut the notches on the left of the stencil.
2 Set out the spacing for the design on the wall by

LATE-SUMMER SEEDHEAD FRIEZE

positioning the stencil at the left-hand side of the frieze. Use the water-soluble crayon to mark the position of the right-hand side of the stencil on the skirting board and on the paper masking. Move the stencil along until its notches are lined up with these registration marks. Make two more marks where the right-hand edge of the stencil now is. Continue in this manner along the wall.

Resist

1 Spray the back of the stencil with adhesive and place it in its first position.

2 Cover the area all around with paper for protection, then spray the beeswax resist into the stencil (see p. 150).

3 Remove the stencil from the wall and clean off excess wax from the front of the stencil using absorbent kitchen paper. To do this, lay the stencil down on a smooth surface – a Formica-topped kitchen table would be ideal – and dab the wax off, ensuring none goes on the back of the stencil.

4 Reposition the stencil in the next-but-one position, using the crayon registration marks and the notches to guide you. Spray with wax again. Continue along the wall in this manner, cleaning up the stencil each time you use it, until you have completed every alternate position on your frieze. Leave to dry (2–3 hours). If there is any wax on the wall which is still wet at this point, blot it off carefully with absorbent paper but do not rub it or the wax will spread where you do not want it to go.

5 Repeat steps 1–4 on the remaining alternate sections.

Shadows

1 Mix up the shadow colour in the screw-top jar. Place half of the mixture in the large container and put to one side.

2 Clean the stencil thoroughly, then reposition it on the wall half the width of the stencil to the right of its original position. Set out the registration marks in the new position.

3 Pour a little of the shadow colour onto a saucer, then lightly sponge and rub in the paint. Move the stencil along the wall as before and repeat the sponging. This will create the shadows of the seedheads which appear behind and to one side of the resist images. Allow to dry (30 minutes).

❷ DUSKY MAUVES
The colours in this swatch have been made from 2tbsp white, 2tsp dioxazine purple, 1tsp ultramarine and ½tsp black applied as in the basic recipe over trowelled-on white emulsion. This is a rather more subdued solution for a smart interior.

❶ GOLDEN HAY
The basic recipe gives a warm sunny design that will brighten a room even when the sun is not shining.

❸ SAGE AND LEMON
Here, a wash of 10tsp hansa yellow light diluted with water as in the basic recipe was applied before the wax resist. The shadow colour – also the base for a second wash – is 10tsp white, ¼tsp phthalocyanine blue, 1tbsp raw umber and ½tsp payne's grey.

colourwash

1 Use the remaining shadow colour to make a colourwash in the ratio 4 parts water : 1 part paint. Use the two decorators' brushes to colourwash the whole of the frieze (see pp. 124–5), then leave to dry (15–20 minutes).

2 Soak a soft rag in white spirit and rub the motifs quite firmly to remove the wax. As you do so, you will reveal the background colour which the beeswax will have tinted a warm, amber white. Don't overdo the rubbing if, like us, you prefer to leave a little texture on your motifs.

protective coat

To protect your work, you should wax it by applying polish with a lint-free cloth. Finally, remove all the masking and you will have completed your field of seedheads casting their shadows on your wall.

FRUIT-MACHINE
COUNTER FRONT

Generally, all-over designs on walls must not be too busy or they will dominate a room, but in many homes there are small areas that can be given more adventurous treatment. This design, inspired by a fruit machine, was chosen partly because of the ease with which the motifs could become large, simple stencils. We were quite playful with the design, but aimed for some sophistication because of the counter's location in a dining area. Hence we abandoned the normally garish colours of the fairground in favour of a more subdued palette. The effect was enhanced by sponging the colours on, leaving some of the background showing through.

BASIC RECIPE – MULTICOLOURED

PREPARATION

Prepare the surface thoroughly. See pp. 24–7.

INGREDIENTS

For a counter front up to 3m² (32ft²)
Base coats ▶ 400ml white vinyl matt emulsion / 1tsp each yellow ochre and cadmium yellow artists' acrylic colour
Motifs ▶ (artists' acrylic colours used throughout)
Stripes ▶ 4 tbsp white
Plums ▶ 2tbsp white / 1tsp dioxazine purple / 1tsp ultramarine blue
Lemons ▶ 2tbsp white / 4tsp yellow ochre / 1tsp cadmium yellow
Cherries and stars ▶ 1tbsp white / 4tsp yellow ochre / ½tsp naphthol red
Lucky sevens ▶ 2tbsp white / 2tsp yellow ochre / 1tsp phthalocyanine blue / 1tsp payne's grey
Bells ▶ 2tbsp white / ¼tsp black / ¼tsp phthalocyanine blue

EQUIPMENT

1 x 200mm (8in) medium-textured roller plus paint tray / container / 7 saucers / 1 large and 6 smaller pieces household sponge / tape measure / spirit level / water-soluble crayon / masking tape / tracing paper / pencil / paper / stencil card / repositionable spray adhesive / scalpel / cutting mat / string / 5 screw-top jars

FRUIT-MACHINE COUNTER FRONT

INSTRUCTIONS

Base coats

1 Use the roller to apply half the white emulsion to the counter front. Allow to dry (2–4 hours).

2 Pour the remaining emulsion into the container and add the yellow ochre and cadmium yellow. Stir well. Spoon some of this mixture into a saucer and, using the large sponge, apply evenly to the counter front, leaving little flecks of the white base coat showing through (see p. 130). Allow to dry (2–4 hours).

Layout

1 Divide the counter front into groups of three bands, as you would see on a fruit machine. On our counter, the three 420mm (16½in) wide bands for the motifs are separated by 50mm (2in) wide white stripes. There is a 70mm (2¾in) wide white stripe at each end of both sets of three bands, and a 50mm (2in) wide gap at the centre. Mark all the lines with the water-soluble crayon and use a spirit level to check that they are vertical.

2 Mask out for the white stripes (see pp. 40–1). Spoon the white stripe colour, a little at a time, into a saucer, and apply using a small sponge.

Stencils

1 Cut your stencil card to the width of the widest bands. Trace the stencil images on p. 218, enlarge them on a photocopier and use them to make the stencils (see p. 36), ensuring that the images are placed centrally before cutting. Do not forget to include the notches from the images. These will act as registration marks, enabling you to line up the stencils correctly.

2 The stencilled motifs are positioned along horizontal lines 300mm (12in) apart. To mark for these, stretch a piece of string from one side of the counter to the other, making sure it is the same distance from the floor at each end. Place masking tape at the points where the strings cross the white lines. Repeat for all the horizontals.

3 Spray the back of the first fruit stencil lightly with adhesive and position it between the white lines, with its notches lined up with the masking-tape horizontals.

4 Mix each of the motif colours in a screw-top jar. Matching the paint to the stencil, spoon some of the colour you are going to use into a saucer. With a small sponge, stencil the motif on as evenly as possible (see p. 37), but allowing the base coat to show through a little. Remove the stencil, then repeat using each of the other fruit stencils.

5 Repeat using the bells, lucky sevens and stars stencils in the same way and with their respective paints.

6 To achieve the shadows on the fruits, reposition each stencil, then lightly sponge on the second colour, taking care not to overload the sponge with paint. Beginning at the bottom edge of each fruit, dab the colour on lightly. Keep your sponge on the move and, as it dries out, move it in towards the centre so that the colour fades out gradually. Reload your sponge as necessary, but take care not to overdo the shading or it will look too heavy. The plum is shaded using the blue of the bells, the cherries in the plum colour and the lemon with the cherry colour.

7 The bells, lucky sevens and stars do not have shadows. Instead, frame them, using the final stencil which is, in fact, a half-frame. First position the stencil to make the upper half of the frame, and then the lower half. The sponging leaves no joins. The sevens are framed in the cherry red, the stars in the plum colour and the bells in the yellow of the lemons.

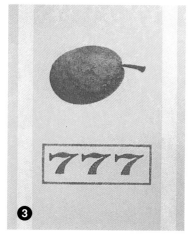

❶ CHERRIES AND BELLS
The cherries use a mixture of white, yellow ochre and naphthol red, and are shaded with the plum colour. The bells are sponged in a mixture of white, black and phthalocyanine blue, and are framed in the lemon yellow.

❷ STARS AND LEMON
The lemon is sponged in a mixture of white, yellow ochre and cadmium yellow, and is shaded with the cherry colour. The stars use the cherry red and are framed in the plum colour.

❸ PLUM AND SEVENS
The plum is made of white, dioxazine purple and ultramarine blue, and is shaded with the blue of the bells. The lucky sevens are a mixture of yellow ochre, white, phthalocyanine blue and payne's grey, and are framed in the cherry red.

DAISY-STREWN
FLOORBOARDS

We wanted this floor to look as if it had been strewn with giant flowers by a passing nymph. It may look like a difficult project, but there is no need to be discouraged. Thanks to the use of sponging and large, easy-to-use stencils, you could complete it in a day. The arrangement of the flowers is very casual and can be made to fit any shape or size of room. Our flowers are set within a rectangular border, which gives the look of a carpet, but one or two small groups of flowers would also be effective. The design is best suited to old, characterful floorboards, but it could be used on any floor. A concrete floor, for example, could well benefit from a gentle carpet of flowers, to add a layer of softness to an otherwise austere surface.

BASIC RECIPE – DAISY WHITES ON GREEN

PREPARATION

Prepare the surface thoroughly. See pages 24–7.

INGREDIENTS

For a floor approximately 9m² (97ft²)
Basic green ▶ 125ml white vinyl matt emulsion / 1tsp phthalocyanine green artists' acrylic colour / ½tsp payne's grey artists' acrylic colour / ½tsp raw umber artists' acrylic colour / water in the ratio 2 parts water : 1 part colour
Basic grey ▶ 250ml white vinyl matt emulsion / ¼tsp payne's grey artists' acrylic colour
Petals ▶ 8tbsp white artists' acrylic colour
Yellow tinge ▶ 4tbsp basic grey / ½tsp cadmium yellow medium artists' acrylic colour / ½tsp yellow ochre artists' acrylic colour
Mauve tinge ▶ 4tbsp basic grey / scant ¼tsp dioxazine purple artists' acrylic colour
Blue tinge ▶ 4tbsp basic grey / scant ¼tsp ultramarine artists' acrylic colour
Flower centres ▶ 5tbsp hansa yellow light artists' acrylic colour / ¼tsp payne's grey artists' acrylic colour
Stalks ▶ 8tsp basic green / ½tsp payne's grey artists' acrylic colour / ½tsp phthalocyanine green artists' acrylic colour
Border ▶ 8tsp basic green
Protective coat ▶ 2 litres matt acrylic or polyurethane floor varnish

EQUIPMENT

Tape measure / straightedge / large set square / masking tape / newspaper / large container / 7 screw-top jars / 1 x 150mm (6in) decorators' brush / tracing paper / pencil / paper / water-soluble crayon / repositionable spray adhesive / stencil card / scalpel / cutting mat / 7 saucers / 4 household sponges and 3 smaller pieces / artists' hog-hair fitch / 1 x 150mm (6in) varnish brush

DAISY-STREWN FLOORBOARDS

1 Mark out the perimeter of your design with masking tape. Protect any areas that are not to be painted with newspaper, also taped down.

2 Mix up the basic green colour in the large container and set aside 16tsp of it in one of the screw-top jars. Make up a colourwash with the remainder in the ratio 1 part water : 2 parts colour. Use the decorators' brush to wash colour lightly onto the unmasked area. Do not attempt to cover all the wood in one coat – keep it loose and leave some gaps. A second coat will cover any bare wood, but for the best effect you should deliberately aim for an uneven finish. Allow to dry (2–4 hours).

Layout

1 Trace the designs for the flowers on p. 219 and enlarge them as necessary on a photocopier to suit the dimensions of your own floor.

2 Plan your design by scattering the photocopies across the floor until you have a layout you find pleasing, then mark their positions with the water-soluble crayon.

Flowers

1 Use the photocopies to cut your stencils (see p. 36), but do not discard the 'positives' as you will need them later to act as masks.

2 Spray the back of each flower stencil lightly with the adhesive, then place them in position and mask out the centres with their positives.

3 Spoon some of the petal colour into one of the saucers and use it to sponge in the flower stencils. You should aim for a soft, misty effect.

4 Round off the ends of three pieces of sponge, to make dabbers about 20mm (¾in) across.

❶ **DAISY WHITES ON GREEN**
The basic recipe. Here the design has been stencilled in the same colours as on page 188, but onto new floorboards, so the colours do not sink in so readily. It has also been varnished with an acrylic varnish which does not darken the wood so much, dries very quickly and, being water-based, is safer and more pleasant to use.

❷ MOODY MAUVES ON GREEN This swatch is more robust in its colouring. For the background colourwash you will need 125ml white emulsion, 4tbsp raw umber, 3 tbsp payne's grey and 2tbsp phthalocyanine green diluted with water as in the basic recipe. Each flower's petals are sponged in one of three colours: (i) 2tbsp dioxazine purple, 2tbsp white and 1tbsp raw sienna; (ii) 2tbsp purple,1tbsp ultramarine and 2tbsp white; or (iii) 2tbsp each purple, white and quinacridone red. These petals have all been tinged with the same colour – mars red freely dabbed on. The flower centres and stalks use the same colour as the basic recipe, and the flicks are in quinacridone red.

5 Mix the basic grey in another screw-top jar and use it as the base for each of the petal tinges. Mix all the remaining colours and store each in its own jar. When you need to use a colour, spoon some into a saucer and dab your sponge in it.

6 With the flower stencils still in place and the centres still masked out, use the dabbers to apply patches of tinge colour (one colour per flower) at the inner ends of the petals. Continue across the floor, varying the colours as you go. They do not have to be exactly the same since these are wild flowers, not show specimens. Leave to dry (30–60 minutes).

7 Now position the stencils for the flower centres, masking off the petals with their positives. Sponge the centres in with their colour. Do this quite loosely and coarsely. Leave to dry (30–60 minutes).

8 Position the stalk stencil for each flower, placing it at varying angles to create the scattered-flower look, and sponge in with its colour.

9 Use the same colour to add random flicks of green around the flower centres, applying them with the artists' fitch.

Border

Finally, create the border. To do this, add a line of masking tape 25mm (1in) in from the tape marking the perimeter. Sponge this border in with the remaining basic green.

Protective coat

Remove all masking and leave to dry for two or three days. Using the varnish brush, apply two or three coats of matt acrylic or polyurethane floor varnish according to the manufacturers' instructions. If you opt for a varnish which requires two chemicals to be mixed together, check that it is compatible with water-based paints.

ARTS AND CRAFTS
STAIRCASE

For this project, as many of you will recognize, we took the set of nine squares which so often feature in the work of the Scottish architect and designer of the early twentieth century, Charles Rennie Mackintosh, and painted them up a flight of stairs and around a landing. The strong rectilinear structure of the design makes for an effect that is crisp and contemporary. We also wish to acknowledge our indebtedness to the inventor of masking tape, since this project, along with many others we have done for this book, would have taken a whole lot longer to paint if we had not used it.

BASIC RECIPE – DARK GREY AND STONE

PREPARATION

Prepare the surface thoroughly. Since the risers on a staircase often get kicked, they will benefit from a coat of primer. See pp. 24–9.

INGREDIENTS

For a 10-step staircase plus a half-landing
Risers ▶ 300ml ready-mixed off-white vinyl matt emulsion
Border ▶ 180ml white artists' acrylic colour / 3tbsp raw umber artists' acrylic colour / 1tbsp yellow ochre artists' acrylic colour
First square colour ▶ 4tbsp black artists' acrylic colour / 2tbsp white artists' acrylic colour / 4tsp burnt umber artists' acrylic colour
Second square colour ▶ 2tbsp white artists' acrylic colour / scant ¼tsp raw umber artists' acrylic colour
Protective coat ▶ 1 litre acrylic varnish

EQUIPMENT

25mm (1in) masking tape for delicate surfaces / paper / scalpel or scissors / 2 x 50mm (2in) decorators' brushes / 3 screw-top jars / fine-grade sandpaper / tape measure / thin card / pencil / 2 saucers / 2 pieces household sponge / 1 x 6mm (¼in) paintbrush / 1 x 75mm (3in) varnish brush

INSTRUCTIONS
Risers

Protect the treads with masking tape and paper, then apply two coats of colour to the risers using a decorators' brush. Allow 4 hours for the first coat to dry, then leave the second coat to dry overnight. Remove the tape and paper.

Border

Using more masking tape, mask off a border 110mm (4½in) wide down each side of the stairway and around the edge of the half-landing. Mix up the border colour in a screw-top jar and, again using a decorators' brush, apply two coats of paint to the border, allowing 4 hours between coats. Sand

down each coat after it has dried, but extend the drying time of the final coat as long as possible. The next stage requires you to use a substantial amount of masking tape, and the harder the paint, the less chance there is of it being lifted off when you remove the tape. We were quite firm with our final sanding as we wished to create a flat and slightly worn look to this paint layer in order for it to blend in well with the wood of the stair.

Squares

1 In this design, each riser is decorated with six squares and each tread with nine, all in rows of three. The pattern continues around the landing. Each of the squares is 45 x 45mm (1¾ x 1¾in) and is separated by the width of the masking tape. You may need to adjust the size of your squares to fit the dimensions of the stairway you are working on. Mark out the design using masking tape to create the squares (see p. 41). You will need plenty of tape and a lot of time for the masking, but it will be worth the investment of both. You can speed things up by making a 'ruler' or template from a strip of thin card, the width of a square. Mark the 'ruler' with a row of three squares, spaced and positioned as they will be on the stairs. Use this to mark out the treads and risers for the masking tape. You can make a longer 'ruler' to suit the dimensions of your landing.

2 Mix up the two colours for all the squares in the remaining screw-top jars. To use each colour, place a little of it on a saucer and dab the sponge into it (see p. 130). Begin by sponging the first square colour on each tread and riser, but leave one square unpainted on each. You should vary the position of these unpainted squares from riser to riser, and from tread to tread. Similarly, as you sponge in the squares around the landing, leave one square unpainted in every block of nine.

3 On completion of the first colour, sponge in the unpainted squares with the remaining colour. This creates a little non-conformity in the otherwise symmetrical design.

4 Remove all the masking tape with care. If any paint has bled beneath the tape, scratch it off with a scalpel and touch it up with a small paintbrush.

5 Allow to dry for two days, protecting the stairway with clean paper if it is in use.

Protective coat

Apply a minimum of three coats of varnish according to the manufacturers' instructions.

❶ DARK GREY AND STONE
The basic recipe.

❷ STONE AND POWDER BLUE
The risers are as in the basic recipe. The border is 225ml white emulsion, 1tbsp cobalt blue and 1½tsp yellow ochre. The first square colour is half the border colour from the basic recipe, and the second square colour is 2tbsp white, ¼tsp cobalt blue, ¼tsp yellow ochre and ¼tsp payne's grey.

❸ DEEP RED AND DARK SLATE
The risers are as in the basic recipe. The border is 135ml black, 4tbsp white and 3tbsp burnt umber. The first square colour is 100ml naphthol red and 1tsp payne's grey. The second square colour is 2tbsp of the border colour from the basic recipe.

SEAWEED AND SHELL CUPBOARD

Milk paints, if you can find them, would be attractive for these cupboard doors, and if you have an old home and prefer to use traditional paints, they would be the ideal choice. Unfortunately, they are not widely available, but many manufacturers make an acrylic-based, matt-finish paint that could be used in their place. We have chosen our paints from a range developed to look like milk paint in finish and colour, and we found it to be a successful alternative. Whether it will be as durable as the real thing remains to be seen.

BASIC RECIPE – ANTIQUE WHITE WITH SAGE

PREPARATION

Prepare the surface thoroughly. See pages 24–7.

INGREDIENTS

For 3 large cupboard doors
First colour ▶ 300ml sage 'milk' paint
Second colour ▶ 300ml antique white 'milk' paint
Third colour ▶ 1tsp dioxazine purple artists' acrylic colour / 1tsp neutral grey artists' acrylic colour
Border squares ▶ ¾tsp phthalocyanine green artists' acrylic colour / 1½tsp neutral grey artists' acrylic colour / 1tsp white artists' acrylic colour

EQUIPMENT

2 x 50mm (2in) decorators' brushes / 2 x 100mm (4in) decorators' brushes / tracing paper / pencil / paper / 3 pieces stencil card / repositionable spray adhesive / scalpel / cutting mat / tape measure / water-soluble crayon / 3 saucers / 2 household sponges plus 2 rounded-off pieces / fine-grade wet and dry paper / bucket of water / 1 x 6mm (¼in) square-ended artists' brushes / tiny, fine natural sponge

INSTRUCTIONS
Background

1 Using the decorators' brushes, apply two coats of the first colour to the doors. Begin with the panels, then follow up by painting first the cross rails, then the stiles. Finish each section by brushing out the paint in the same direction as the grain. We have also painted the panelling surrounding the doors. Allow 1–2 hours for each coat to dry.

2 Apply two coats of the second colour in the same way.

SEAWEED AND SHELL CUPBOARD

Stencils

1 Trace the designs on p. 219, enlarge and use to make the first stencil – the wavy rectangles with the seaweed – and the second stencil – the registration marks and the shell motifs (see page 36).

2 Position the first stencil in the centre of the door panel, holding it in place with the spray adhesive. Sponge on some of the first colour using a trimmed household sponge (see p. 37). Remove the stencil and repeat the process on the other doors. Leave the paint to dry overnight.

3 Using the wet and dry paper with water, lightly sand the doors, including the stencilled areas and the mouldings. Avoid removing too much paint from the stencilled areas and do not rub the paint back beyond the first colour (see p. 152–3). Rinse the wet and dry paper frequently in a bucket of water, and use a sponge to mop up the slurry of paint. Clean up well with a fresh sponge and plenty of fresh water.

4 Position the second stencil on one of the doors, using the registration marks to line it up with the first stencilled motifs. Sponge on the second colour, again using a trimmed sponge, and applying the colour a little unevenly to create highlights. Remove the stencil and allow to dry (2 hours). Repeat on the other doors.

5 Cut out from the third piece of stencil card the registration marks and the line details of the shells (see p. 219). Do not cut the lines for the border yet. Position this stencil over the already-stencilled motifs, lining it up with the registration marks on each corner.

6 Mix the third colour on a saucer, using an artists' brush to blend the paints together. Using a tiny natural sponge (synthetic ones are too coarse), stencil in the details – not too evenly – with this colour. Remove the stencil and allow to dry (30 minutes). Repeat on the other doors.

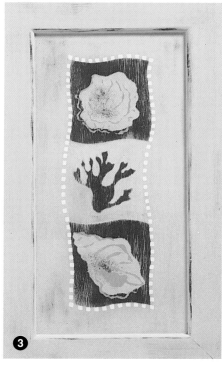

❶ ANTIQUE WHITE WITH SAGE
The basic recipe. The antique white and pale sage green showing through suit this room beautifully. Although the room is in a French seaside town, it has taken on a Scandinavian air.

❷ SKY BLUE WITH ANTIQUE WHITE
Here we have painted two coats of sky-blue 'milk' paint – a total of 300ml – over two coats of antique white – also 300ml. The third colour, for the stencil details, is a mixture of 1½tsp white, and ¼tsp each burnt sienna and burnt umber. The border squares are in 4tsp white plus ¼tsp phthalocyanine green.

❸ PRIMROSE YELLOW WITH AUBERGINE
We began with 300ml aubergine 'milk' paint, followed by 300ml primrose yellow. The third colour is a mixture of 1½tsp white and ¼tsp each phthalocyanine blue and neutral grey. The border squares are a lighter version of these colours, made by doubling the quantity of white.

Border

1 Cut the lines for the border out of the third stencil. Reposition this, and use as a template to draw in the border.
2 Mix the border squares colour on a saucer and use a square-ended artists' brush to paint in the small squares between the marked border lines. Make sure that you end up with a square in each corner.

PAINTED PANES ON
A PART-GLAZED DOOR

If you are looking for an alternative to net curtains or blinds, painting a window may be the answer. It can be more than just a device to distract your eye when there is a less than pretty view on the other side. Painting a window is also a lovely way to filter the light that passes through it and, on bright sunny days, the colours of the paint will be projected into the room, which can be uplifting, summer or winter. A painted interior glass door will also bring colour into a room that changes as the daylight fades and lamps are switched on.

The windows on these pages were decorated with a paint designed to give the appearance of coloured or stained glass. It was bought from an artists' suppliers. Once it has hardened, you can clean the glass with a soft cloth, but use only the mildest of detergents.

We wanted to stencil the design and found the best material to make the stencil was self-adhesive plastic film attached to the glass before the motifs were cut out from it. It sticks firmly to the glass, but can be removed easily. We had first tried using acetate and met with some success, but even though the acetate was attached with spray adhesive, the very liquid paint seeped underneath, leaving us with a very messy clean-up operation.

After painting the glass, we chose a harmonizing yellow colour to paint the door frame.

BASIC RECIPE – SKY BLUE AND OLIVE

PREPARATION

Prepare the surfaces thoroughly. See pages 24–7.

INGREDIENTS

For an average window
First colour ▶ 50ml sky blue glass paint
Second colour ▶ 50ml olive green glass paint
Door frame ▶ 5tbsp white vinyl matt emulsion / 2tbsp yellow ochre artists' acrylic colour / 3tbsp hansa yellow light artists' acrylic colour / 2tsp raw umber artists' acrylic colour

EQUIPMENT

Tracing paper / pencil / paper / clear acetate (optional) / glue stick / repositionable spray adhesive / transparent self-adhesive plastic film / scalpel / masking tape / 2 saucers / 2 small, rounded-off pieces household sponge / container / 1 x 50mm (2in) decorators' brush / 1 x 25mm (1in) decorators' brush

INSTRUCTIONS

Layout

1 Trace the spiral and leaf motifs on p. 219 and enlarge them on a photocopier, making several copies. Arrange them into a design that will fit your door. On our door we decorated a top and bottom row of panes. Each pane was

divided into three equal bands, with the motifs in each reversed from pane to pane. To make the reversed motifs, photocopy them onto acetate and turn the copies over. If acetate is not available, tape photocopied motifs back to front on a window, and pencil over the image seen. On our door, the upper panes had leaves in the top two bands and spirals in the lower band. The lower panes had spirals in the top band and leaves in the lower two bands. The instructions that follow are for panes with spirals in the top band.

2 Once you have planned your design, glue the individual motifs in position on a sheet of paper that fits your panes and attach to the glass with a light spray of adhesive.

Stencil

1 Cut pieces of transparent self-adhesive plastic film to the exact size of your window panes and attach them to the front of the glass. This plastic film is to become your stencil.

2 Using a scalpel, cut carefully along the lines of the design as seen through the glass. (A word of caution: the point of the scalpel will leave lines scratched on most types of glass. These will not be visible after the painting as the edges of the paint will coincide with them, but if you subsequently decide to remove the paint, they will show. To avoid this, you can cut the stencils from the plastic film before you stick it down, but be warned that this is a much more fiddly procedure.)

3 Peel away the following sections of the stencils: from the lower band, peel off the background, leaving the leaf shapes in place; from the middle band, peel away the leaves, leaving the background in place; from the top band, peel away the background, leaving the spirals in place. You will now be left with stencils attached to your glass, which the glass paint cannot get behind.

4 Protect the door frame around the glass with masking tape, then starting with the middle band, also mask off below the leaf stems to prevent the colour seeping into the lower band.

5 Pour a little of the first colour into a saucer. Use a small piece of sponge to apply the colour to the leaves in the middle band. Sponge the colour out in one go until you have an even texture (see pp. 168–9). Allow to dry (4 hours).

6 Remove the masking from below the stems and protect the work you have just completed with masking tape laid

❶ SKY BLUE AND OLIVE
The basic recipe. This rather Mediterranean colourway would bring a warm glow to any room.

GREY AND TURQUOISE
Here the central leaves have been stencilled in grey glass paint, and the two outer bands in turquoise. To make the colour for the door frame, mix ½tsp each phthalocyanine green and burnt umber into 180ml white emulsion.

delicately across stems and leaf tips, where they touch the top and bottom bands.

7 Pour a little of the second colour into a saucer and with a fresh piece of sponge, apply it to the top and bottom bands, sponging out as before. Allow to dry (4 hours).

8 Remove the plastic-film stencils and masking tape from the door frame to reveal your design crisply painted on the glass. At this stage it will still be a little delicate, but it becomes harder after a few days.

Door frame   Mix the paint for the door frame in the container and use the decorators' brushes to apply two coats, allowing 2–4 hours for each coat to dry.

JAPANESE FABRIC
SCREEN

This project combines rugged builders' props with a light, translucen
fabric. It would make an excellent solution to screening off an area of a
room for those of you who do not wish to use more traditional screens
When choosing a site for your screen, ensure that the ceiling is solid
enough to take the upward force of the props. If possible, locate
the screen below a beam. There will be no need to over-tighten the
props as they will only be supporting the fabric, not the building.

BASIC RECIPE – RAW SIENNA AND NEUTRAL GREY ON CREAM

PREPARATION
Prepare the surface thoroughly. See pages 24–7.

INGREDIENTS
For a screen 2 x 1.4m (6½ x 4½ft)
**Screen ▸ 2 x 1.5m (6½ x 5ft) dark cream roller-
blind fabric / 4m (13ft) double-sided adhesive
tape / 2.2m x 12mm (7ft x ½in) diameter metal
rod / 2m x 12mm (6½ft x ½in) diameter metal
rod / 2 adjustable builders' props to suit your
room size
First colour ▸ 2tbsp raw sienna artists' acrylic
colour
Second colour ▸ 2tbsp neutral grey artists'
acrylic colour
Lines ▸ 2tbsp white artists' acrylic colour
Optional ▸ aerosol can silver paint**

EQUIPMENT
**2 large pieces stencil card / 25mm (1in) wide
(minimum) masking tape / straightedge / pencil /
500mm (20in) string plus pin / scissors / tape
measure / repositionable spray adhesive / 3 large
pieces household sponge / 3 saucers / paper /
offcuts of padding (see Notes)**

INSTRUCTIONS
Stencil

1 The design is made up of three large motifs, each
stencilled using the same 600mm (24in) diameter stencil.
Since stencil card rarely comes this big, you will have to join
two pieces of card together. To do this, lay the two pieces flat
on a table or on the floor with their edges butting up
together then stick masking tape down the join on both
faces of the card.
2 Use the straightedge and a pencil to mark the diagonals of
the card and, to draw the circle, pin the end of the string at
the centre of the card where the diagonals cross. Pull the

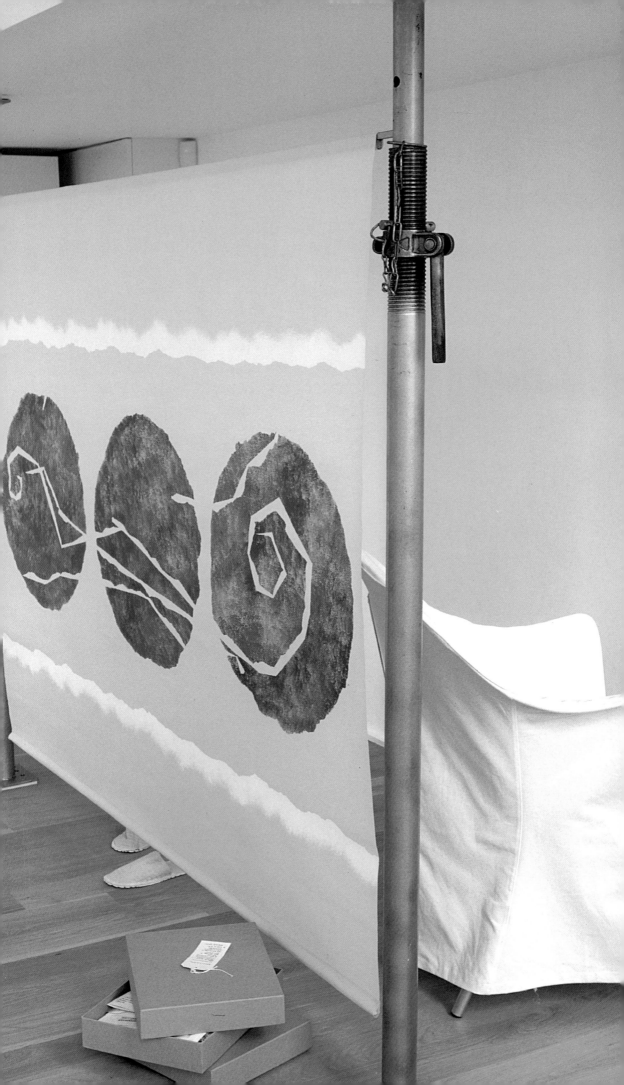

string tight and attach the pencil 300mm (12in) from the pin using masking tape. Place the pencil point on the card and sweep it round the pin, keeping the string taut. Do not worry if the circle you end up with is less than perfect.

3 Make a hole in the stencil card with the scissors, then carefully tear the card along the line you have drawn to remove the circle.

Motifs

1 Lay the roller-blind fabric out on a flat surface. Use the floor if you do not have a large enough table. The motifs are stencilled horizontally across the centre of the fabric, with 50mm (2in) spaces between. Measure out and mark for the positioning of the motifs using small pieces of masking tape. Do not use pencil or crayon as these marks will be difficult to remove from the fabric.

2 Spray the back of the stencil with adhesive and place it in its first position.

3 To make the lines that run through the circles, firmly stick small strips of masking tape torn along their length to the fabric framed by the stencil. Build up the design following the examples shown here.

4 Trim two of the pieces of household sponge into balls using scissors. Spoon a little of each of the first and second colours into separate saucers and use the rounded pieces of sponge to apply them to the fabric. The textured effect is created by sponging on the two colours at the same time and letting them overlap in places. There is no need to blend them into one another.

5 Remove the masking tape and the stencil and allow to dry (20 minutes).

6 Repeat, placing the stencil in its second and third positions. For each new motif use fresh masking tape, positioned so as to continue the linear element of the design.

Lines

1 A sponged white line runs 150mm (6in) above and below the row of circles. The inner edge of each of these lines is masked off with segments of torn paper (see p. 42). The outer edge is faded off with the sponge. Use a long straightedge laid on the fabric as a guide to position the first torn-paper mask. Spoon some of the white paint into

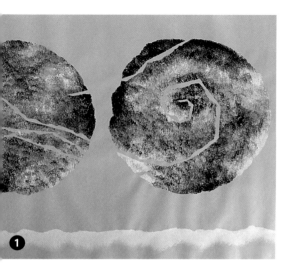

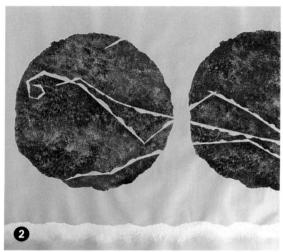

another saucer and use a sponge to apply it along this edge, fading the colour away to make a line approximately 50mm (2in) wide. You are not aiming for a line of a perfectly constant width. Remove the masking paper and allow to dry (20 minutes).

2 Repeat for the second line, allowing 1 hour to dry.

Making the screen

1 Turn the stencilled fabric over and stick half the double-sided tape to the top edge. Lay the longer rod on the tape, leaving 100mm (4in) protruding at each end. Roll the fabric over and around the rod, fixing it in place with the tape.

2 Repeat using the shorter rod for the lower edge of the stencilled fabric.

3 If you feel as we did that the adjustable props need smartening up, spray them with the spray paint, following the manufacturers' instructions.

4 Now you will need some help. Adjust the props to the height of your room and fix one prop in position, ensuring that the holes in its inner sliding section face inwards. Slot the longer rod of the screen into one of these holes at the desired height, making sure that the screen is facing the right way round.

5 Move the second prop into place, pushing it along the floor until the rod slides into the corresponding hole on this prop. Fix the second prop in position and your screen is finished and in place.

Notes Builders' props are not the most delicate of objects and can leave marks on your floor and ceiling. Avoid this by using padding. Offcuts of foam rubber, cork or carpet would all be suitable.

❶ ACHROMATIC The first colour uses 2tbsp payne's grey and the second 2tbsp white in addition to the 2tbsp white for the two lines.

❷ COBALT BLUE AND TERRACOTTA The first colour is 2tbsp cobalt blue and the second is 2tbsp mars red. The white lines are as in the basic recipe. This recipe gives a more colourful version.

MOCK-SLATE
COFFEE TABLE

Slate slabs look wonderful but would be too heavy for a table that is sometimes moved around. They are also expensive. Our alternative – mock slate produced with artists' acrylic colour that is burnished as it dries – overcomes both these problems. We took the opportunity to combine it with a painted design. For our basic recipe, we applied it in a deep sea blue to a wooden surface, but there is no reason why it could not be applied in other colours to other surfaces, garden pots for example or stencilled motifs on a conservatory wall.

BASIC RECIPE – DEEP SEA BLUE AND SLATE GREY

PREPARATION | Prepare the surface thoroughly. See pages 24–7.

INGREDIENTS |
For a coffee table
Base coat ▶ 100ml white vinyl matt emulsion
First colour ▶ 2tbsp payne's grey artists' acrylic colour
Second colour ▶ 1tsp phthalocyanine blue artists' acrylic colour / 1tsp phthalocyanine green artists' acrylic colour
Slate undercoat ▶ 100ml black vinyl matt emulsion
Slate topcoat ▶ 5tbsp payne's grey artists' acrylic colour / 1tbsp white artists' acrylic colour / 1tbsp phthalocyanine green artists' acrylic colour / 2tsp burnt umber artists' acrylic colour
Lines ▶ 1tsp neutral grey artists' acrylic colour / ½tsp mars black artists' acrylic colour
Burnishing ▶ small tin of furniture wax or beeswax
Protective coat ▶ 1–2tbsp furniture wax

EQUIPMENT | Small, smooth paint roller plus tray / fine-grade sandpaper / tape measure / water-soluble crayon / 2 saucers / 3 household sponges / bowl of water / 3 screw-top jars / paper / repositionable spray adhesive / 1 x 50mm (2in) decorators' brush / flexible spatula / medium flat artists' brush / lint-free cloth

INSTRUCTIONS
Base coat | Use the smooth roller to paint the whole table top with the emulsion. This will leave a fine, smooth texture. Allow to dry (4 hours), then sand lightly.

Cross | Our table measures 1200 x 450mm (48 x 18in). The long arm of the cross on it is 60mm (2½in) wide, and the short arm is 140mm (5½in) wide. The dimensions of yours will depend on the size of your table. Using a tape measure and the water-soluble crayon, roughly sketch out the cross, drawing it 50mm (2in) larger all round than the finished design. Do not

MOCK-SLATE COFFEE TABLE

forget to extend the arms of the cross over the edges of the table as we did.

First and second colours

1 Spoon a little of the first colour onto a saucer and sponge it loosely into the cross. There is no need to attempt to sponge a neat edge as this will be created at a later stage. Before the paint dries, splash and flick water onto it, then sponge off with a clean, damp sponge to leave a variegated texture (see pp. 131–2). Allow to dry (1 hour).

2 Mix up the second colour in a small screw-top jar and spoon a little onto a saucer. With a clean, barely damp sponge, rub a transparent layer of this colour over the first. Allow to harden (1 hour).

Masking

1 Again using the water-soluble crayon, lightly redraw the cross, this time to the exact dimensions. Mask off the cross using torn paper held in place with spray adhesive (see p. 41). If you tear the paper along its grain, it will give the cross its straight, soft edges. Again, do not forget to extend the arms of the cross over the edges of the table.

2 Using the decorators' brush and the slate undercoat, paint in the four exposed rectangles of the table top. Allow the paint to dry (4 hours).

Burnishing

1 Mix together the colours for the slate topcoat in another screw-top jar. Use the spatula to apply this mixture to a small area of a painted rectangle. Create the polished-slate look by

burnishing the paint. To achieve this, use small, circular movements of the spatula while the paint dries. As the paint becomes tacky, add a little wax to the surface and continue burnishing. The wax makes it easier to manipulate the spatula and also forms part of the hard, polished, slate-like finish as it is driven into the paint. Add more wax as and when you need it.

With practice, you will be able to judge when the paint is dry enough to be burnished, as well as what slight changes you can achieve in the patina by variations in your timing, waxing and burnishing.

Work across the surface of the table in this manner and do not stop

❶ DEEP SEA BLUE AND SLATE GREY The basic recipe.

❷ VENETIAN RED AND SLATE GREY Here, the base coat, the first colour and the slate undercoat and topcoat are as in the basic recipe. The second colour is 2tsp magenta and 1tsp burnt sienna, while the lines are painted using 1½tsp neutral grey.

❸ DARK YELLOW AND SLATE GREY Again, the base coat, the first colour and the slate undercoat and topcoat are as in the basic recipe. The second colour uses 2tsp hansa yellow light and ¼tsp neutral grey, and the lines are painted using a mixture of 1tsp neutral grey and ¾tsp white.

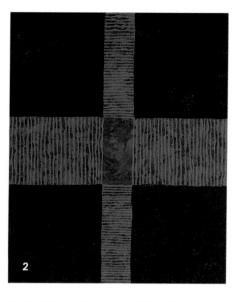

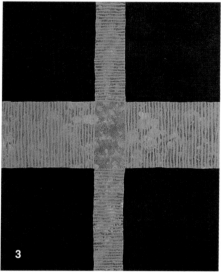

until you have completed a whole rectangle. Treat the edges of the table in the same way. The whole procedure will take some time, but it is not arduous and there is great satisfaction to be gained from watching the surface texture form beneath the spatula.

2 Remove all the paper masking and leave the paint to harden thoroughly overnight.

Lines

Mix up the colour for the lines in another screw-top jar and use the artists' brush to paint them across the arms of the cross. Twist the brush a little as you paint in order to create variations in their width. Note that the central section of the table does not have any lines. Allow to dry for a day.

Protective coat

Use a soft, lint-free cloth to wax the whole table.

CHEQUERBOARD
TABLE TOPS

Table tops, providing they are finished with a protective coat to prevent them getting damaged during use, are the ideal surface for many of the decorative paint techniques we use in this book. These chequerboard table tops are another example of what can be achieved. If we had painted a regular chequerboard pattern on them, they could have been used for playing draughts, but we decided to throw in an asymmetric section which varies from table to table. You will find that the squares-within-squares are easy to mark out and apply. You will also be able to adapt them to suit any size of table. And if you do not have a table, then just paint a board of the size you want, and set it on the biggest wheels you can find.

BASIC RECIPE – SAGE ON RED

PREPARATION　　Prepare the surface thoroughly. See pp. 24–7.

INGREDIENTS　　*For a small side table*
Base coat ▶ 6tbsp white vinyl matt emulsion
First colour ▶ 2tbsp payne's grey artists' acrylic colour
Second colour ▶ 1tbsp magenta artists' acrylic colour / ½tbsp alizarin crimson artists' acrylic colour
Green checks ▶ 4tsp white artists' acrylic colour / 1tsp phthalocyanine green artists' acrylic colour / 1½tsp payne's grey artists' acrylic colour / 2tsp raw umber artists' acrylic colour
Beige checks ▶ 2tsp white artists' acrylic colour / ¼tsp raw umber artists' acrylic colour
Grey checks ▶ 2tsp payne's grey artists' acrylic colour
Protective coat ▶ 3tbsp matt or satin acrylic varnish

EQUIPMENT　　1 x 75mm (3in) decorators' brush / fine-grade sandpaper / 4 saucers / 4 household sponges / bowl of water / 2 screw-top jars / ruler / water-soluble crayon / 2 x 10mm (⅜in) flat artists' brushes / 1 x 50mm (2in) varnish brush

CHEQUERBOARD TABLE TOPS

INSTRUCTIONS
Base coats

Using the decorators' brush, apply two coats of white emulsion, allowing 4 hours for each coat to dry. Sand down lightly between coats and after the last coat has dried to remove any bits of hardened paint or dust, otherwise they may show up later as white spots in the finished surface.

First and second colours

1 Spoon the payne's grey onto a saucer and sponge it loosely onto the table top and sides (see p. 130).
2 Immediately splash the surface with water, then use a clean sponge to sponge off some of the grey paint, leaving a heavily variegated texture (see pp. 131–2). Allow the paint to dry (1 hour).
3 Mix together the magenta and alizarin crimson on a saucer. Dip a clean, damp sponge into this mix and rub it into the surface, leaving a transparent coating over the grey. Your table top should now look like an exotic piece of polished marble. Allow to dry (1 hour).

Painting the checks

1 Meanwhile, mix up the colours for the checks.
2 Mark a chequerboard grid on the table top, using the crayon. Aim for squares with sides of approximately 50mm (2in). Each of our designs is different although all are based on a common grid. In this example, a group of twenty-one squares has been subdivided into smaller squares.
3 Using the artists' brushes, paint the squares, the alternate larger ones in green and the smaller ones in beige and

payne's grey. Spoon a small amount of each colour on a saucer and load your brushes from there. If the paint does not flow smoothly, you may need to add a little water.
4 As you complete every two or three squares and before they dry, flick or splash a little water over them, as you did earlier. Leave for a moment, then press a clean, damp sponge onto the squares to create the texture seen in the example. Don't forget to paint the edges.
5 Set your table aside for a couple of days after finishing it to allow the paint to really harden off. Using the varnish brush, apply a minimum of two coats of varnish according to the manufacturers' instructions.

❶ SAGE ON RED
The basic recipe.

❷ DUSTY MAUVE ON EMERALD
Our second table top, which is predominantly green, is started in the same manner as the first. The first colour is 2tbsp payne's grey. Two coats of phthalocyanine green, a total of 2tbsp, are rubbed into it to make quite a dark tone. The larger checks are painted in a mixture of 4tsp white, 2tsp ultramarine, 1tsp payne's grey and ½tsp magenta. The subdivided checks are painted with 2tsp mars red and 2tsp payne's grey.

❸ DUSTY MAUVE ON LIME
The third table top begins again with a sponged-on base coat of white emulsion, followed by a coat of 2tbsp payne's grey as the first colour. A thin coat of 1tbsp hansa yellow light is rubbed into that. This gives a lovely depth to the painted surface, reminiscent of marble, though it must be said it is not a marble you are likely to find in a quarry. In this design, a line of larger checks has been added, crossing from one side to the other. The blue checks are in the same blue as the checks in recipe 2, while the green checks are in 2tsp green from the basic recipe, and the red checks are painted using 2tsp mars red.

MOTIFS & TEMPLATES

The majority of the motifs we have used in our designs have been drawn out here for you to trace. Many of them will have to be enlarged or reduced to the size you would like them, but this can be done easily on a photocopier. Note that some include registration marks which must not be omitted when tracing or enlarging, as they are essential to the correct placement of the motif in a design.

Pages 137–8: An ornate stamp

Pages 142–3: Oak-leaf border

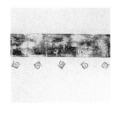

Pages 144–5: Simple border

Pages 147–8: Stippled panels

Page 149: Painted-wax resist

Pages 157–8: Overlapping stencils

Pages 160–2: Seaside doors

Pages 163–5: Fossil table design

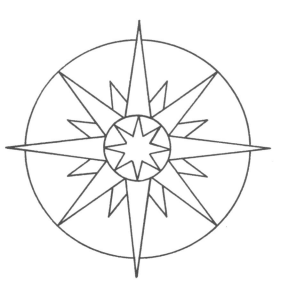

Pages 166–7: *Rose des vents*

Pages 168–9: Painting on glass

Pages 180–3: Late-summer seedhead frieze

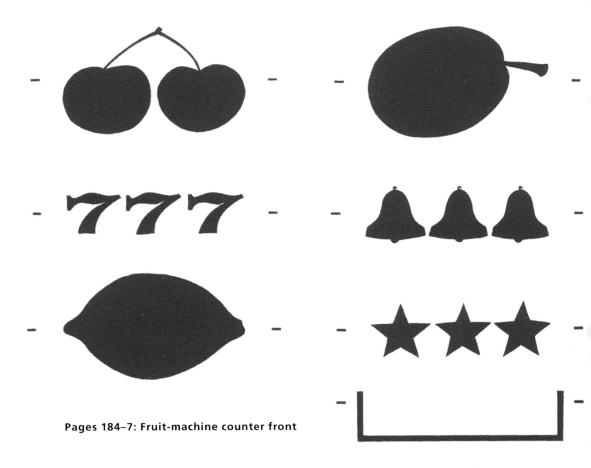

Pages 184–7: Fruit-machine counter front

Pages 196–9: Seaweed and shell cupboard

Pages 188–91: Daisy-strewn floorboards

Pages 200–3: Painted panes on a part-glazed door

LIST OF SUPPLIERS

Most of the tools and material used in this book are available from DIY stores or artists' suppliers. Should you find difficulty obtaining any item, consult the following list of specialist stockists, suppliers and manufacturers. Many manufacturers will give advice on their products, supply catalogues, and may send goods by mail order.

⊠ indicates that a mail-order service is available.

Acrylon Environmental Ltd
P.O. Box 84
Amersham
Buckinghamshire HP6 6DX
01494 726890
Manufacturer and supplier of water-borne coatings for ferrous metal, galvanised steel, fibreglass, masonry and wood

Auro Organic Paints
⊠
Unit 1
Goldstones Farm
Ashdon
Saffron Waldron
Essex CB10 2LZ
01799 584888
Suppliers of natural paints, including linseed oil-based, and other ecologically sound water-based paints

J. W. Bollom
⊠
Unit 1
Croydon Road
Beckingham
Kent BR3 4BL
020 8658 7723
Manufacturer of sign-writers' glass paints, oil scumbles, pigments, as well as of general supplies for the decorator. Stockists of masking tape for curves

Lawrence T. Bridgeman
⊠
1 Church Road
Roberttown
Liversedge
West Yorkshire WF15 7LS
01924 413813
Supplier of a range of paints based on American vintage colours and recipes, including a simulated buttermilk paint

Brodie and Middleton Ltd
⊠
68 Drury Lane
London WC2B 5SP
020 7836 3289
Supplier of artists' colours powder pigments and metallic powders, specialist brushes, and theatrical textiles and sheet materials

Cornelissen and Son Ltd
⊠
105 Great Russell Street
London WC1B 3RY
020 7636 1045
Manufacturer and stockist of artists' and gilding materials. A long-established company with a large stock of traditional products

Craig & Rose ⊠
172 Leith Walk
Edinburgh EH6 5EB
0131 554 1131
Manufacturer and supplier of acrylic scumbles, glazes and varnishes

Daler-Rowney Ltd
12 Percy Street
London W1A 2BP
020 7636 8241
Retailer of fine art and graphics products

Farrow & Ball ⊠
33 Uddens Trading Estate
Wimborne
Dorset BH21 7NL
01202 876141
Manufacturer known especially for their excellent range of paints developed for the National Trust, including floor paints in many colours. Primarily a mail-order company

Grand Illusions ⊠
2–4 Crown Road
St Margarets
Twickenham
Middlesex TW1 3EE
020 8607 9446
Orders (Dorset)
01747 854092
Manufacturer and supplier of acrylic-based paint that emulates milk paint

Green and Stone ⊠
259 King's Road
London SW3 5EL
020 7352 0837
Supplier of artists' materials, crackle varnishes, all paints (including milk) and scumbles

John Jones Art Centre
⊠
Stroud Green Road
Finsbury Park
London N4 3JG
020 7281 5439
Supplier of all manner of artists' materials and equipment; also customised framing. Excellent products and service

Leyland Paint
SigmaKalon
Huddersfield Road
Birstall
Batley
West Yorkshire WF17 9XA
01924 477201
Manufacturer of paint, varnishes, glazes, artists' colours, specialist decorators' materials, brushes and tools. Excellent products and services. Stockists in London and throughout the country

Liberon Waxes
Mountfield Industrial Estate
Learoyd Road
New Romney
Kent TN28 8XU
01797 367555
Manufacturer of gold waxes and coloured waxes for wood

John Myland Ltd ⊠
80 Norwood High Street
West Norwood
London SE27 9NW
020 8670 9161
Supplier of sandpapers, wood finishes, waxes, varnishes and paints

Nutshell Natural Paints
⊠
Mardle House
Mardle Way
Buckfastleigh
Devon TQ11 0NR
01803 762329
Supplier of powder pigments

Paintworks Ltd ⊠
99–101 Kingsland Road
London E2 8AG
020 7729 7451
Supplier of a wide range of artist materials, including environmentally-friendly paints, varnishes, pigments and wood treatments.

Paper and Paints Ltd
⊠
4 Park Walk
London SW10 0AD
020 7352 8626
Supplier of a wide range of specialist and traditional materials and equipment

Plasterworks ⊠
38 Cross Street
Islington
London N1 2BG
020 7226 5355
Manufacturer and supplier of architecural cornices

E. Ploton Ltd ⊠
237 Archway Road
London N6 5AA
020 8348 2838
Supplier of artists', gilders' and decorators' materials and equipment

Polyvine Ltd ⊠
Vine House
Rockhampton
Berkeley
Gloucestershire GL13 9DT
0870 787 3710
Manufacturer of water-based products, including frosting varnish for glass, scumbles, floor finishes and pigments

Potmolen Paint ⊠
27 Woodcock Industrial Estate
Warminster
Wiltshire BA12 9DX
01985 213960
Manufacturer of traditional water-based paints and materials, brushes and pigments

Stuart Stevenson ⊠
68 Clerkenwell Road
London EC1M 5QA
020 7253 1693
Supplier of artists' gilding materials and equipment

Col Art Fine Art & Graphics Ltd
Whitefriars Avenue
Harrow
Middlesex HA3 5RH
020 8427 4343
Manufacturer of artists' paints, materials and equipment. Stockists nationwide

INDEX

INDEX

ACKNOWLEDGMENTS

TEXT ACKNOWLEDGMENTS

Text on the following pages by Liz Wagstaff: 12–19, 46–93, 96–119.
Text on the following pages by Lynne Robinson and Richard Lowther: 9–11, 20–22, 24–7, 30–43, 94–5, 122–215.

PICTURE ACKNOWLEDGMENTS

The publisher wishes to thank the following photographers and organizations for their kind permission to reproduce the photographs in this book:

48 Elizabeth Whiting & Associates; 51 Mick Hales; 58 The Interior Archive/Christopher Simon-Sykes (artist: Celia Lyttleton); 60 The Interior Archive/Simon Brown (designer: Christopher Gollut); 68 Arcaid/Richard Bryant (Costa Careyes Villa, between Puerto Vallarta and Nanzamillo on the Mexican Pacific Ocean); 76 © Trevor Richards/Homes & Gardens/IPC Syndication; 83 The Interior Archive/Simon Brown (designer: François Gilles); 87 Elizabeth Whiting & Associates/David George; 89 Elizabeth Whiting & Associates/David George; 90 Paul Ryan/International Interiors (designer: Shinbach); 98 Arcaid/Ken Kirkwood (Penhow Castle, Gwent); 107 Paul Ryan/International Interiors; 112 Elizabeth Whiting & Associates/Andreas von Einsiedel.

All the special photography was by Debbie Patterson, with the exception of the verdigris garden fountain on page 109, which was photographed by Linda Burgess. Studio photography of paint samples, materials and equipment was by Nicki Dowey (pages 9–11, 20–2, 24–5, 30–32, 34–43, 94–5, 125, 127–9, 131–3, 135–9, 141, 143, 145, 147–51, 153–5, 157–60, 162, 164, 167, 169, 175, 179, 183, 187, 190–1, 195, 199, 203, 207, 211, 215) and Patrick McLeavey (pages 12–19, 28, 49, 53, 55, 57, 59, 61–5, 67, 69, 71–5, 77–8, 81–2, 86, 88, 91, 93, 97, 99–102, 104, 106, 108, 113–4, 116, 119). The paint roller illustrations are by Clive Goodyer.